Our Time of Day

KIKA MARKHAM

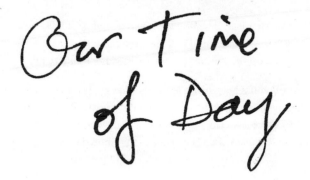

Our Time of Day

My Life with Corin Redgrave

OBERON BOOKS

LONDON

First published in 2014 by Oberon Books Ltd
521 Caledonian Road, London N7 9RH
Tel: +44 (0) 20 7607 3637 / Fax: +44 (0) 20 7607 3629
e-mail: info@oberonbooks.com
www.oberonbooks.com

A catalogue record for this book is available from the British Library.

PB ISBN: 978-1-78319-100-0
E ISBN: 978-1-78319-599-2

Front cover image by Edward Webb
Back cover image by Terry Johnson

Printed and bound by Replika Press Pvt. Ltd., India.

For Corin

CONTENTS

Preface   1

PART I

Chapter 1 Our Parents   6

Chapter 2 Politics   13

Chapter 3 France   21

Chapter 4 On my own   27

Chapter 5 Billingsgate   32

Chapter 6 A Proposal   34

Chapter 7 New Zealand   36

Chapter 8 Difficult Times   42

Chapter 9 *Haddock à l'Anglaise*   45

Chapter 10 Moving Theatre   58

Chapter 11 Perugia   75

PART II

Chapter 12 **June 2005** Corin Collapses   80

Chapter 13 **June 2005** Different Hospitals   87

Chapter 14 **Summer 2005** Corin Comes Home   103

Chapter 15 **August 2005** Springfield   114

Chapter 16 **October 2005** Rehab   124

Chapter 17 **October 2005** Back to Work   134

Chapter 18 **Summer 2006** Holiday Breaks   140

Chapter 19 **February 2007** Our Mother Dies   144

Chapter 20 **August 2007** No Future?   152

Chapter 21 **March 2008** AA   157

Chapter 22 **March 2009** Going On   169

Chapter 23 **Summer 2009** Memories   175

Chapter 24 **April 2010** Goodbye   182

Chapter 25 **May 2010** Highgate Cemetery   187

Four Years Later   190

Acknowledgements   193

Sources   195

List of Plates   196

Index of Names   197

Preface

Kika's diary

Tuesday 23 June 2009

Rehab session with Dr B

We were talking about Corin's increased drinking and the fact that he often drank alone. Whether he missed his past activities, responsibility, socialising etc. What did we miss about one another? Dr B addressed the question to me: '…communication, we often spoke four times a day, more when we were apart… he looked after me'.

The doctor asked Corin the same question. 'Communication, yes…'

'Why do you enjoy going to Paris?' she asked.

'Well, the wine.'

'Just the wine?'

'Yes, the variety, the pleasure of going to a wine shop… and choosing.'

'What else did you like about Paris?'

'Well, just sitting in a café with a glass of wine…'

I thought he must say: 'Kika and I were happiest there, in our flat, going to old movies, shopping in the market in Boulevard Raspail', but no, nothing…

'Can I say something?' I asked. 'You see I don't think Corin remembers our life at all before the heart attack, therefore there's nothing to want to go back to that other life for, or to stop drinking for, if he doesn't regret or wish to be together again or long for the happy times.'

'Is it true Corin that you don't remember your life with Kika?'

'Yes it is true, I mean I know we were happy. And I know I loved Kika, but I can't remember our life together.'

So what I had always dreaded and feared was in fact true. This was the first time that it had ever been acknowledged by either of us in a 'clinical' situation, and so honestly and simply, by my husband. Now I understood that both our lives had disappeared. For what use are memories if they only exist for one person? My memories were already shrivelling and dying inside my head. The only way that they could be kept alive was by sharing them. I was trying to keep my face normal, not grimace and howl. There was a silence. I could feel a tear falling out of my left eye, although my face was like granite. I picked up my newspaper, folded it noisily and took some gulps of water from the plastic cup.

Four years later as I read this I realise that, in fact, he had remembered the most important thing of all, our love for one another.

'This is a common thing', Dr B said after a pause, 'have you ever looked at photographs together? It might be helpful.'

We agreed it would be a nice thing to do.

It was the end of the session and we walked to the car.

'Well here's a situation! There is a married man who has had a heart attack and four years later admits to his wife that he has no memories of their life together and that she could be an imposter for all he knows. What about that for your next play?' I said in a horrid jovial voice.

'That's a brilliant idea, I could start writing almost immediately... Why not indeed?!' answered Corin, as we drove down the leafy streets of Wimbledon in the summer evening.

So I turned it into an anecdote, which became the impulse for starting this book.

I never meant this to be a book, just a way of recording events so that at least these memories would be kept for both of us. It would be mine and Corin's account of an extraordinary journey. I hope too, that it will bring comfort and help to people that have suffered or lived with brain injury.

Kika Markham

Part I

CHAPTER ONE

Our Parents

Corin and I were halfway through our lives before we realised that we loved each other, although our paths had crossed many times and we were always aware of each other's presence, however distant. In fact, researching for this book, I came across an interview Corin gave for *The Times* (1995) where he says 'She [Kika] spent a great deal of her time on activities that bring people blisters on their feet and bring cold comfort. It made me love her from a distance.'

Our parents had become friends even before we were born, when they worked together at Liverpool Playhouse (before the Second World War). My mother Olive knitted a blanket for Rachel Kempson's second baby, Corin, and Rachel knitted a cardigan for my mother's 'expected any day' second baby, me. Michael Redgrave, Corin's father, and David Markham, my father, had worked together in a film about the struggle of the miners in the 1930s: *The Stars Look Down*, based on the novel of the same name by A.J. Cronin. Corin wrote about it in his book *Michael Redgrave: My Father*:

> ...the man on the screen [Michael Redgrave] is thirty-one, not much older than my eldest son [Luke] – and in his cloth cap and shirt-sleeves, his long wrists too long for his jacket, his long neck and half-awkward movements, he looks and sounds not much more than a youth. Stranger still, the young man who plays the son of the coal owner is David Markham, my wife's father; and David looks even younger.

Both Corin's and my parents were radical. My mother had written a poem against Hitler for *Punch* magazine while a teenager in Munich in 1935, and had been deported by the Nazis who had intercepted it. My father David was sent to prison for being a conscientious objector. Michael Redgrave was thirty years old when he announced to the *Liverpool Echo*, 'I am a red-hot socialist, I believe in everything to do with Socialism'. As Corin wrote, 'It was not unusual for a leading actor to say that in those days, although it would be today'. Both David and Michael had friends that were fighting and dying in the Spanish Civil War. Marxism was popular. Michael signed up for The People's Convention, a socialist document, which ultimately had him banned from working for the BBC. David signed the People's Pledge, which called for the renunciation of all wars. But his views were not straightforward pacifist ones.

In 1940, David registered as a conscientious objector, and was permitted conditional status providing he did forestry and ambulance driving as part of the war effort, which he agreed to. He was then offered a job with the Old Vic Theatre Company by the great visionary director Tyrone Guthrie, touring the UK with the Council for the Encouragement of Music and the Arts (CEMA) and this meant the authorities couldn't always find out where he was. According to the account of the Ministry of Labour, in a wartime letter typed on the front and back of flimsy paper, my father refused a medical examination and was then summoned to a tribunal. Tyrone Guthrie supported him in a letter dated 14 May 1942:

> [David Markham] has frequently been employed by the Old Vic as an actor in classical plays. I think highly both of his talent and of his character.
>
> Although I, personally, do not agree with his objection to National Service, I believe it to be sincere; and I hope that he may be allowed to continue to use his considerable talent and technical experience as an actor.
>
> In this event, I would be prepared to offer him continuous work with the Old Vic, under the sponsorship of the Council for the Encouragement of Music and the Arts. The latter, it

will be remembered, is financed by the Treasury through the Board of Education. This work is recognised by the Ministry of Labour as being of national importance.

It is, I think relevant, that the Old Vic does not work for private profit, and that Mr Markham's salary, since the war, has always been arranged, at his own request, at a figure which covers his expenses, but is quite incommensurate with his value in the commercial theatre, or, for that matter, with his value to the Old Vic.

My mother wrote about their experience in a book by Jonathan Croall, *Don't You Know There's a War On? Voices from the Home Front*:

> Tyrone Guthrie was very good to him ... But managements were certainly very unsympathetic, it was all doing things for the troops. Also David couldn't do those war films at all. He said they were made to show how wonderful war was and just romaticized it. He refused to act in Noël Coward's *In Which We Serve*, which annoyed Coward, who then circulated all the studios, saying that David was difficult and shouldn't be employed ... The Reading tribunal was very bad, they were very anti. But David's way made it difficult for the judges to decide that it was a conscientious objection. It wasn't religious, you see ... The judge, who was almost asleep, gave him six months at first, but then somebody behind prodded him and said, "The maximum sentence is a year, my lord." And he woke up and changed it, and said, "A year's hard labour."
>
> David then went to Winson Green prison in Birmingham. I remember we had a horrible goodbye ... The other prisoners were terribly kind to him. There was a gang of housebreakers who were very nice; the leader said he would teach David how to break into a house afterwards, he'd show him how to open windows, and then he could join the gang ... He was in Winson Green for two months. Wormwood Scrubs, where he was

transferred to, was better, there was more communication, and it was generally easier ... When he came out he was completely grey, and he couldn't talk. He had had flu and jaundice, and he just spoke in a whisper, which was horrible.

My father's beliefs caused great difficulties in the families. Both of my parents' brothers had fought in the war, and one of my uncles, Howard Harrison, was an RAF pilot and was shot down, but survived. Not one of them ever said a bad word about Dad. A testimony to his humanity and sweetness, and their kindness. But my mother says her father never forgave David.

Growing up under the weight of such sacrifice on many levels had a sobering effect on me. In family discussions, words and phrases like 'Ambition', 'Successful career', were used in mocking terms, whereas 'Failure' seemed to be more honourable. Both Corin and I had a sense of responsibility towards our fathers, which we only became fully aware of in retrospect.

After the war Dad became a prison reformer, mainly working with Radical Alternatives to Prison (RAP). He also formed the Campaign Against Psychiatric Abuse (CAPA), which led to years of fighting for the release of a young Russian student, Vladimir Bukovsky, standing, often alone, in all weathers outside the Russian Embassy. My sisters and friends took turns to stand with him but to my bitter regret I never did. Other members of the campaign included Harold Pinter, Peggy Ashcroft, Iris Murdoch, Peter Hall, François Truffaut and George Steiner. When Bukovsky was finally freed he stayed for a night in my parents' room at our home, and it became known as the 'Bukovsky room' for ever more.

Without the spirit of my parents, Lear Cottage has returned to being an ordinary, small, red-tiled East Sussex cottage, but while they were alive, extraordinary attributes – almost mythical – were attached to it. It lay tucked away in the middle of Ashdown Forest a mile away from A.A. Milne's house, held in place by a field on either side and a stream that ran alongside it. Hidden from the outside world by the surrounding forest of bracken, heather gorse, brown streams and pine trees, the cottage became a refuge for anyone in need of comfort. My mother invited one of the Guildford Four down to recuperate following her release from prison after one of the most notorious miscarriages of justice in recent times, and they remained lifelong friends.

My father kept rare breeds of pigs and poultry, which he loved to show at Smithfield, the biggest livestock show in the UK, held at Earls Court. We never had more than one or two pigs at a time and they all became pets. Ada, the golden-haired Tamworth, being the most admired. We took her acorn hunting through the forest, sometimes greatly alarming family picnickers. We had a red Dexter cow, Gloria, who provided us with butter, milk, and cream with which my mother made legendary strawberry ice cream, cakes and puddings when she wasn't writing stories or poetry. There were dogs and cats, guinea pigs, rabbits, ducks and hens and a pony and trap we used for picking up stray guests from the bus stop.

My father played the violin and I was learning the piano so when I got good enough we played Mozart, Beethoven and Schubert violin and piano sonatas, only choosing the slow movements which we could just about manage without arguing. We laughed a lot and played to an audience of sleeping dogs and cats in the tiny sitting room, which was so dark in the day you could barely read the music. At the end of a piece, we sometimes heard, 'That was nice!' My mother's voice floated from the kitchen.

The cottage and the forest were of great solace to me and my sisters. There were four of us: Sonia, me, Petra and Jehane. Soon after we started to live there, we were, one by one, packed off to weekly boarding school. Me aged seven, Sonia aged nine. It was like being cast out of Eden. How could our kindly 'free-thinking' parents have decided on such – to my mind – brutal separations? My father's explanation was that his public school had traumatised him, it had been far worse than his experience in prison. Though Olive was equally unhappy at boarding school, she had made a close friend – Jo MacKeith – with whom she formed the Purple Thumbnail Society, which got them through. My parents believed only an alternative educational system, run on the lines of A.S. Neill (Summerhill School) would be beneficial. They were suspicious of any traditional day school which might use the strap, and besides my father wouldn't have been able to get us to school on time having driven back to Sussex each night from the West End, where he was acting.

So they decided that a progressive boarding school would be the kindest solution.

We cried every Sunday night. My first school was only seven miles away but it could have been China for all I knew.

Later we went to a school in Hampstead, called Burgess Hill. In its early days it was an interesting school, even from a child's point of view. There was no uniform and you called the teachers by their Christian names. No one forced you to go to lessons, but the teaching was good so you did.

Children had weekly meetings to discuss problems in the school, which was also effective in dealing with bullying. But later, under a different head, the boundaries between pupil and teacher broke down. As a teenager I got a crush on the art master, and he began a long seduction, kissing me under the water during a swimming lesson at Finchley Pool.

'Is there anything that *could* comfort me?' I asked Dad as he drove Sonia and me to the station to meet the evening train back to school. 'If winter comes can spring be far behind,' he answered kindly.

These dreadful separations were something Corin and I had in common. Corin had been looking forward to boarding school at first. But he writes in his memoir:

> It is quite terrifying to me now, as a father, to review this
> period of my life [he was nine] because I can still remember

its emotions so vividly, to have been among the most turbulent of my childhood. Terrifying, but salutary, because as I read my father's diary I see how little my grief seems to have impinged upon him. And I cannot help accusing myself of the countless times I must have been ignorant of my children's grief.

"Corin said to have been in tears in evening at thought of going back," say his diary on 12 May ... "Corin very upset. Talk to him firmly. Nearly miss train and forget to give him his ticket."

Yes, but I remember that train ride, the most miserable of my life.

And Corin went on to describe his school as a:

hellish, cruel trap, a sort of labour camp, or worse, with remissions, which were the cruellest thing of all, because they gave you a taste of home and its comforts only to tear you away.

In the end, Michael *did* take notice of Corin's grief and took him away, and he went to a day school in London near his home, where he was happy. It was this story of his early unhappiness and of his friend Wilson, whom he had comforted as he sobbed with homesickness night after night that made me fall in love with Corin thirty years later.

CHAPTER TWO

Politics

I left school with very little to show for it except a love of art and literature, two O Levels and a full-blown relationship with the art teacher, for which I was far too young.

My love of literature began early, starting with *Polyanna*, *Little Women*, all of E. Nesbit, all the Brontës, Jane Austen, George Eliot, Virginia Woolf, Katherine Mansfield, Somerset Maugham, Graham Greene, Aldous Huxley, and ending up with D.H. Lawrence, not necessarily in chronological order. Dad read all of Charles Dickens to us in the evenings during the holidays. There was nothing hidden away. Erich Fromm and *The Art of Loving*, Wilhelm Reich, *The Function of the Orgasm*, lay alongside the *Farmers Weekly* and *Farmer and Stockbreeder* on the kitchen table. My father was very interested in Reich and corresponded with him and Bertrand Russell. He arranged for an orgone box to be delivered: invented by Reich to free the individual from sexual repression and prevent cancer, radiation sickness and much else. We were encouraged to take our books with us into the orgone box – the size of a large telephone box – where we sat reading in our vest and pants to get the benefit of the orgone energy. I read with interest that Greg Bellow, Saul Bellow's son also sat in an orgone box, but he used the time to masturbate. Ken Tynan came to have a look at our box; I think he was interested in getting one. Years later Corin played him in a play by Richard Nelson.

Armed with this eclectic mix, I left home and ended up living with the art teacher in two attic rooms in Tottenham Street, and started life as a drama student. At Guildhall School of Music and Drama my status was rather high, not so much due to my talent as to my superior knowledge of contraception.

I wrote a lot of monologues for interviews and auditions, gleaned from listening to the different languages of humans and animals which drifted up from the street below. I was very good at a dog's bark, a bored but unhappy chained-up collie. No doubt an echo of how I felt in my own life. After receiving bemused and amused looks from casting directors I had to give up my idea of becoming a female Percy Edwards (the famous bird and animal impersonator), although Michael Winterbottom used my dog bark in his film *Wonderland*.

After leaving Guildhall I started to get some work – and met Roger Smith, who had written a film script called *Catherine*, and Tony Garnett (who was an actor then and whom I liked very much) – in a short film directed by a (then) newcomer, Ken Loach. This new independence destabilised my domestic situation and the art teacher threw a cup at me across the room, which broke on my right eyebrow. The result was a visit to the Middlesex Casualty Department, which was luckily just around the corner, and fifteen stitches coasting down one side of my right eye. The only person I dared tell was my kind uncle Paul Dehn. An Oscar-winning screenwriter, poet and critic, and my mother's elder brother, close friend of the Redgraves (another coincidence), he and he alone saw the dreadful purple-red, swollen side of my face.

We had tea on his green sofa in Bramerton Street in Chelsea. He was kind and comforting, and pretended not to be shocked, although he must have been. I never told my parents. This horrible event provided me with the impetus to escape from the art teacher, whom my kind parents unwittingly took pity on, taking him with them on holiday to France, whereupon, I recently learned, he made sexual advances to my thirteen-year-old sister.

Later, Tony Garnett introduced me to the Yorkshire playwright David Mercer, who took me out to lunch and then for a walk on Hampstead Heath. He was witty, sympathetic and 'motherly' in a

Yorkshire way. Before long I was living in his flat in Compayne Gardens, above the writer Bernice Rubens.

In those days, the late Sixties, you met a man and, if you liked one another – just liked, not loved – you could be living together within a few weeks, knowing barely anything about them. Shocking to write this now. My only role model had been my mother who, even after having given birth four times, remained determinedly unworldly and beautiful, discarding enhancements like lipstick, bras and high heels, which suited my father very nicely. Although I was already politically active, sitting down in Grosvenor Square in protest over the Vietnam War, marching from Aldermaston to London against nuclear weapons, as a young woman I was profoundly uncertain of myself and could have been the girl Shirley Hazzard described in *The Transit of Venus*... 'fixed. subjected. fatalistic' and waiting... With David I was sometimes required to be a minder as well as his girlfriend. The 'culture of Jimmy Savile' was taken for granted then, and the attitude of men generally and in the entertainments industry was often uncaring, and unprotective towards young women. David was not exploitative, he was very kind but dogged by self-doubt, which made him drink. But it was he who suggested that I see an analyst, seeing a faultline in my 'docility' and passive cooperation, which turned out to be rather helpful.

Long afterwards I found out that David had previously lived with a woman called Dilys Johnson in the same flat. I had obviously taken her place. She might have been his wife. Where had she gone? Was she broken-hearted or relieved? I never found out. I wasn't callous, just young and ignorant and responding to someone who wanted me, and because it was flattering living with a brilliant playwright. I don't know whether he loved me – I wasn't yet sure what love was... or what the convention required was.

David was writing *A Suitable Case for Treatment*. He was a very funny, warm-hearted person, but suffered from depression. I accompanied him to the south of France to stay with Tony Richardson and Oscar Lewenstein. They were working on a new film script, *The Sailor from Gibraltar*. My job was to keep David away from all the booze – so that when a dinner party was to be held we were ignominiously shown the gate and told to come back when it was over. At that unhappy, but nevertheless interesting, time I almost met Corin's sister, Vanessa, who was married to Tony then, but as I wasn't at any of the social functions our paths never crossed. I do remember talking to one very sweet, small girl playing in the grass with a doll who I later found out was Natasha, Vanessa and Tony's eldest daughter.

Back in London David started taking me to Friday night meetings held by the Socialist Labour League. It was there that I developed my interest in Marxism. I felt I was getting educated for the first time in my life, listening to writers like David and Jim Allen. They discussed the Suez Canal, the Vietnam War, the Bretton Woods Agreement, taking the dollar off the gold standard, the crisis of capitalism, and the need for a planned economy, an idea dismissed at the time as a far-left and naïve, utopian fantasy. Today, Thomas Piketty's book *Capital in the Twenty-First Century* analyses why capitalism doesn't and *can't* work any longer. He advocates 'a progressive tax, a global tax based on the taxation of private property'. How interesting that his focus on wealth and inequality mirrors what we were discussing at the time. Despite his rejection of a revolutionary answer, I find it pleasing that his parents were Trotskyists, and took part in the Paris uprising of 1968, as did my parents who took over food to feed the students during the occupation!

I wondered whether socialism could ever be achieved through parliament in Britain. Certainly Trotsky believed it could never happen while the monarchy remained in power. Some years later I was in a TV drama, *A Very British Coup*, based on Chris Mullin's book about an elected prime minister who was not only a socialist, but insisted on carrying out socialist policies – the fact that he was then overthrown by the Establishment fitted in very well with this view, although Chris Mullin was never to my knowledge a Trotskyist. My political education was beginning, and it was utterly absorbing. I was also, reluctantly, learning about the self-destructiveness of man – David – and the effects of alcohol. Nearly every Friday or Saturday night David would go to a dive in Soho called the Pickwick Club. I dreaded the phone call at midnight which would ask me to come and fetch him in a taxi.

I would go downstairs to the dark, smoke-filled room and bar, where shapes lurked and ducked, and would try to spot him, hoping he was not in the arms of another woman – which could happen. Usually he was not, but sometimes he could barely stand and it was a tough job getting him into a taxi. And if it all went very wrong he would become angry and I would sometimes take off out of the house, running down Compayne Gardens in my pyjamas, and hovering around the corner outside the immense red-bricked mansions under the lamplight till I thought he would be asleep.

My parents, always supportive of our boyfriends and often ignorant of the real situation, invited David down to Sussex for one Christmas. They liked him a lot. Mercer was friendly with David Warner, the actor, who was playing Morgan in *A Suitable Case for Treatment*, and had no plans for the holiday. So he came too, along with my sister Petra's boyfriend Keith Johnstone (the legendary teacher of improvisation) and who, Petra told me, liked his cornflakes with warm water. It was a miracle that we all squeezed in round the tiny kitchen table. My father carving the turkey and doling it out as if to a hungry band of very tall, bearded children. Later David, learning my father and I were going to play some music together on the piano and violin, heard my father say 'Come on Kika, let's murder Vivaldi!' and wrote a television play using the phrase as a title. It was about me and the art teacher. A cruel, funny play.

I ran away from David on the night of his premiere in Paris of *A Suitable Case for Treatment*. We were staying at a five-star hotel. I felt very out of place, excluded and jealous as a beautiful blonde French actress was making her presence known to him, which he was enjoying far too much. Karel Reisz, the director of the film, and his wife Betsy were smiling and happy, unaware of my extreme discomfort. Our suite was huge with high, high ceilings and silver chandeliers. There was a giant four-poster bed with a velvet cover and tassels. Marble was everywhere and I hated it. I packed my bag... and disappeared from the hotel. I had remembered that Jehane West was in Paris, staying on her yacht, moored on the Left Bank of the Seine.

An old family friend of my parents, and of the Redgraves, Jehane was godmother to my sister Jehane and an inspiration to us throughout her life. A poet, a sailor and a stage manager, she knew how to live. She was delighted to see me, and we sat on deck drinking tea, watching seagulls catching bread. I don't remember if I went back to the hotel. David had an affair with the actress.

After living alone in Chelsea for a year, I met Malcolm Tierney. He was kind and very funny and said he understood women because he had a sister – which turned out to be more or less true. We lived in a tiny cottage in Peyton Place. There was no hot water, so we went to the public baths once a week, and it was daringly primitive to me. Our life together was happy and adventurous.

To be in politics was inspiring then. It seemed people were ready for a new socialist party, a party that had broken ranks with the communist parties in 1956 and followed Trotsky's analysis, which he outlined in *The Revolution Betrayed*; a permanent, more human vision of socialism. To that end the Workers' Revolutionary Party (WRP) was formed out of the Socialist Labour League, concentrating its energies on theory – the grasping of dialectical materialism – democratic centralism, which I now take issue with. We began a daily paper called *The Workers*

Press which later became *The Newsline*. Each area in London and the provinces had to arrange deliveries of the paper, preferably before people went to work, as well as early morning sales outside factories, tube stations, even the BBC. That could be quite difficult if you bumped into a producer although I used to sell one to John Birt sometimes.

In July there were summer schools held in the country, when comrades discussed the theory of Marxism and were entertained by actors and writers, and we ate on long trestle tables in the open air. Gerry Healy, General Secretary of the party, was beginning to see how important theatre and actors were to a revolutionary movement. Corin had by now become a member but we only met on campaigns or at public meetings.

The commitment required for this new kind of life had a drastic effect on our families. I had dreadfully painful arguments with my father who, from his anarchist perspective, could only see that I was being hopelessly brainwashed. I, on the other hand, was convinced that only the party had the vision to analyse the period that we were living through: that capitalism could no longer be progressive, unrestrained market economics leading to an increase in inequality, social conflict and wars. I hardly saw my sisters. Apparently I stopped talking to them and only talked at them: we were almost strangers. My tone had become hectoring or incredulous when others couldn't see what I was getting at. I don't think Corin's parents were ecstatic about his and Vanessa's involvement either, and it was certainly very difficult for his wife Deirdre as she had no desire to join the party. Their children, Luke and Jemma, hated the smoke-filled meetings held in their flat, and Corin being away for long periods of time.

I had a disturbing encounter with Corin's mother, Rachel, while I was campaigning for union rights for Equity at Granada rehearsal rooms. She spotted me from afar and shouted 'There's that dreadful woman! She's mad and sees a shrink every week [I did] and she's in that awful party that ruined Corin's marriage!' Rachel was a loyal person, and she was extremely fond of Deirdre, as well as adoring my mother – who could never do any wrong in her eyes. She didn't know I was the baby she had knitted a cardigan for, and I didn't know she would end up being my mother-in-law. Some years later, on my first, extremely apprehensive, visit to my future in-laws down at their beautiful cottage in Wilks Water in Hampshire, she welcomed me into the kitchen with the sweetest smile, saying 'Forgive me'.

CHAPTER THREE

France

In the late Sixties I worked at the Royal Court, playing Harriet Shelley in *Shelley* by Ann Jellicoe, Viola in *Twelfth Night*, Abigail in *Time Present* by John Osborne, and, on television, Jane in *The Basement* written by Harold Pinter, who was also in it. Oscar Lewenstein, who worked at the Court then, recommended me to the French film director François Truffaut (*Jules et Jim*; *The 400 Blows*) and Suzanne Schiffman, his close collaborator, for a film called *Les deux Anglaises et le continent.*

I turned up to the interview wearing black, which troubled Truffaut who wondered why I had chosen to dress like a waitress, but I got a screen test and Stacey Tendeter and I were chosen as the two English sisters Anne and Muriel, opposite Jean-Pierre Léaud.

Truffaut had been depressed. The film was planned partly to help his recovery and, little by little, as the filming went on, I became part of that recovery. Difficult as it was to act in another language, I loved working with 'the family', as he called his crew, and with him, and I desperately wanted to please him. I asked my sister Jehane to come out and stay with me as a chaperone to prevent me falling for him. But he was already picking me up after the day's shooting in his sports car, writing me notes, which he would slip under my door, praising my work. It was too late.

I had intended to try to recruit Truffaut into the WRP or, if not that, to get him to finance our paper with a huge donation. I certainly had no intention of getting entangled with him as I had been warned about his fondness for whichever actress he was currently working with. The following story sums up what actually happened. I wrote it two years after the film came out, in the third person for reasons of discretion (Suzanne's instruction), and because it allowed me to be more truthful.

Father Love

'But how did you think it would end – did you imagine marriage?' His voice was gentle, he was trying not to show exasperation.

There was no answer to that, not in her limited French. She was crying on the end of the bed. He swiped at another mosquito with *Le Monde* and fiddled with the shutters.

They were sweltering in a villa in Antibes. The sound of cicadas filled the unhappy silence.

(She should never have come.)

When the film finished, the affair finished. You went home and got on with your 'real' life.

But she hadn't been able to. After listening to all the warnings, she had betrayed her own instincts for self-preservation and had fallen, tumbled, into love with her director.

She went to the south of France to stay with his collaborator and friend Suzanne, who had become her friend too. She hoped the director would find out that she was there and would send for her.

Suzanne had an old farmhouse just outside Vaison-la-Romaine. The garden was a tumbledown orchard leading to vineyards and behind the house a white road crept up to a cemetery and village on top of a hill. She and Suzanne would walk up to the cemetery and pick the thyme that grew on the scrubby banks, and from there they watched purple and black clouds chase birds helterskelter into the trees before the storm. They talked of food, children and politics – anything and everything except the affair and her unhappiness. It would have been bad taste and besides it might have revealed countless other women that Suzanne had befriended in similar circumstances…

Then a letter came.

'Tu est plus vrai que mon cinéma… Viens me voir.'

('You are more real than my film… Come and see me.')

It was a line from the scene where she said to her lover, 'Tu est plus vrai que ma sculpture. (je t'aime)'

('You are more real than my sculpture. (I love you)')

It was a message full of promise but she had misgivings. What would it be like to be with him now the film was over? They had never done anything 'normal' together. The entire relationship had taken place on locations, sets or in hotels. She had never even made a cup of tea for him, would he expect her to cook for him and entertain his guests?

She arrived in Antibes early in the evening. The rented villa looked unfriendly and chic. Clipped hedges arranged themselves around patterns of gravel and the grass was over-watered and looked too green under the dusty fat trees. You could smell and hear the sea but that was all. The hedges had been planted to stop one looking any further. Although his greeting was warm, it seemed he too was unsure of what to do.

He was shocked at her appearance. Perhaps he remembered an image of her in the final scene off the film: pale, black-ringed eyes, dying of tuberculosis. Now she was very tanned and fatter.

As he was working with another writer on his next film script *La nuit américaine* (*Day for Night*), she didn't want to be in the way – so, avoiding various interesting-looking people in the villa, she went and sat on the balcony and tried to read.

She was studying Lenin's *Philosophical Notebooks* and in particular the chapter 'On The Question of Dialectics'.

It was required reading for anyone who was serious about Marxism, which she was:

> The condition for the knowledge of all processes of the world in their "self-movement", in their spontaneous development, in their real life, is the knowledge of them as a unity of opposites. Development is the "struggle" of opposites...

Underneath she had written a quote from Hegel which was now unreadable, smudged by tears which plopped from her chin to her hand and from her hand to the page. Self-pity in all its self-movement and spontaneous development. How horrible.

She had tried to get him to take an interest in Trotskyism. It proved very disappointing. In her limited vocabulary her ideas sounded over-simplified. He remained unconvinced although respectful. He had a strong suspicion of 'organized' politics.

She closed the book and went downstairs. Drinks were on the terrace. Dinner was served. Who cooked the food? There must have been a discreet housekeeper whom she never saw. She couldn't get a grip on herself.

In the morning he told her that he had offered her father a part in the next film. She thought of trying to explain this to her therapist:

'No – don't you see, he didn't want me – he wanted my father.'

Her father had played a small role as a fortune teller, playing a scene with her, in *Les deux Anglaises*, looking at her palm reproachfully… 'You are going to have several unhappy affairs – there is much confusion here…'

'He loves fathers,' Suzanne had told her. 'His own family was such a mess that he thinks everyone else's is wonderful.' So there it was. She had been replaced by her father. He had fallen in love with him.

Who was writing which script?

She left the next morning. He offered to drive her to the airport. He had tried to give her a farewell present. He owned some beautiful old watches but she was too proud and refused to accept one, although later she regretted this. In the end she chose his yellow towel bathrobe: the only scruffy thing he had and it comforted her. He promised to write and hoped she wouldn't be too sad. He was kind and civilised.

She longed to say something devastating that would stay lodged in his memory forever. Suddenly he touched her knee. She was wearing an old black and white mini-skirt. He liked short skirts.

For a moment she thought it might be a sign that he wanted to begin it all over again. Or was he relieved that she was leaving? There was no knowing.

So they continued, he stroking her knee, thoughtfully, the other hand on the steering wheel, approaching Nice in the soft grey dawn of the Mediterranean.

I thought the film was brilliant. It had never occurred to me that a film by Truffaut would not be successful and would be so misunderstood for its observations about love and there was no one I could talk to about it and my sense of rejection. What made it doubly painful was that it broke up my relationship with Malcolm, which I had never wanted to happen.

Meanwhile, Corin was in Paris filming *Sérail*, directed by Eduardo de Gregorio, with Leslie Caron and Bulle Ogier; I think he was having a romance with a French woman and we didn't meet.

Truffaut and my father stayed in touch, his parting gift being to cast Dad as the doctor in *La nuit américaine* in which he shone with wonderful humour, kindness and beauty. It was as if both he and David Mercer wanted to hold on to my father – David had written a wonderful role for Dad in *And Did Those Feet* after he and I broke up. My father's charismatic beauty affected some of my partners. After his death, Corin wrote about him, 'I loved him very much as a fine courageous man… physically the most beautiful and handsome man I ever saw.'

CHAPTER FOUR

On My Own

I rented a room in Glebe Place, Chelsea. I was getting a lot of work but I felt out of place. Every time a plane went over, I wondered if it was going to, or coming from, Paris. I had trouble crossing roads and panic attacks. I went back to my analyst.

Dennis Potter wanted to meet me; he had writer's block and wanted to discuss a new idea about acting versus prostitution – over a dinner. He had seen me in a commercial for Cornetto, and thought, as a committed socialist and serious actress, I should not have allowed myself to become sexualized for money. I did have doubts myself at the time, but we sold a lot of papers in the pubs on the strength of my being recognised as the 'Cornetto girl'. I went along to meet him at The Regent Palace Hotel and we had a very long, mostly friendly argument for the whole meal, about acting and prostitution. 'How much would I compromise my principles if I got a large fee?' He put it all in the play, everything I said, without taking any notes, and told me that I would play the actress *and* the prostitute – although it would involve doing a nude scene, which I wasn't keen on. But as he believed 'actresses were prostitutes in disguise,' he thought I would agree in the end. And of course I did because it was a wonderful play, although I suffered doing the nude scene and had to suck a Cadbury's Flake. The play was called *Double Dare* and was produced by Ken Trodd for the BBC. I think it's one of Potter's best.

I had started going out with Clive Merrison, and now, thanks to him, I stopped looking up at planes and started to be able to cross roads again. He came with me to France as I made another French movie, this time with Jacques Rivette, called *Noroît*, a film with Geraldine Chaplin and Bernadette Lafont, two great actresses.

Les deux Anglaises opened in London to cool reviews, which was a shock. Nevertheless, I was photographed by Lord Snowdon along with other promising young British actresses for *The Sunday Times*. I had breakfast at Kensington Palace with my friend Francis Wyndham, the writer, and Snowdon before we did the shoot. Possibly the only time a Trotskyist got to sit in a royal kitchen... but these were interludes in my life of ever-increasing political activism.

There were quite a few actors in the party by now, and we were engaged in a campaign to change the rules of Equity so it could be a trade union instead of an association. There was fierce opposition to this as many actors thought we shouldn't be political as entertainers. Corin led the way, inspiring many young actors with his brilliant speeches in theatres where we had our meetings, and using the example of the actors suffering under apartheid in South Africa: banned, unable to work and often in prison. We became a trade union and Corin helped negotiate a minimum wage for actors for the first time. Simon Callow described those days:

> [Corin] suggested that I might like to come to a meeting of the Workers' Revolutionary Party (WRP), offering, almost *en passant*, a concise and dazzlingly lucid analysis of the terminal contradictions of capitalism. He was charm itself – steely charm, but charm nonetheless. Some sense of self-preservation kept me out of the Party, but in somewhat cowardly fashion I made regular financial contributions to it, which ensured that whenever I met Corin I would receive one of his brilliant, slightly lopsided, smiles.

> The next few years brought a much-touted Battle for the Soul of Equity, in which the great casting director in the sky had secured the dream team of, on the Left, Corin Redgrave, lean, dangerous, incorruptible, and, on the Right, the actor Marius Goring, white-haired, patrician, softly spoken, clubbable,

slightly sinister. The battle raged, Equity meetings were a monthly Armageddon, and then Margaret Thatcher pulled the plug on it all by abolishing the closed shop, after which Equity was finished as a political force. Corin threw himself ever more into the WRP, which was plagued by paranoia and a sense that its moment in history had passed. But he worked superhuman hours to advance the cause, down at the docks at 6.00 a.m. to sell the paper, across the country to address a meeting, on the phone at 2.00 a.m. to forge links with foreign comrades. And all the while he was making a living, or trying to, plying the family trade … [I]t was only when his father died in 1985 that he was able to come into his own as an actor, which he did almost immediately, evincing a strength, a warmth and a power that had not hitherto been his to command. It took the world a little while to wake up to the fact that a great actor had arrived, but when it did there seemed to be no holding him back.

It was, nonetheless, with a certain trepidation that I called him to ask him to play the Duke of Windsor in my production of Snoo Wilson's play *HRH*. Snoo's Duke was a skittish silly ass with a penchant for music hall. Would this newly formidable actor want to let his hair down? "Corin," I said, taking a deep breath, "do you by any chance play the ukulele?" "Simon," he replied, "I've been waiting my whole life to be asked to."

As a child, it appeared, he had been obsessed by George Formby, and knew his entire repertory. Then he said: "I do have a suggestion." My heart sank: what Marxist perspective did he want to introduce? "I've always wanted to play the bagpipes on stage, too. Could we work that in?" I said that we could, and we did, and the rehearsal period was as entertaining a time as I've had. Corin proved himself to be a superb light comedian, and sometimes rehearsals had to stop while we laughed till we cried.

In 1973 we were working on an ambitious project, 'The Road to Workers' Power', a dramatised history of early trade unionism. Five directors would each take a team of actors with them into different parts of England and, with the help of the local community, would assemble a cast to enact a part of their history. I was allotted Jarrow, with Steve Clark-Hall, and the story of William Jobling, the last man in the North East to be gibbeted. Corin was in Manchester, doing the Chartist Movement – he must have been playing his renowned Octavius Caesar for the RSC at the time, commuting from Stratford. Roy Battersby was in Wales – Taff Vale – and Roger Smith was in London – The First International and Marx.

In-between rehearsals and recruiting people to take part, we would be selling the paper in the early mornings. I would be at the great Swan Hunter shipyards at 6.00 a.m. as the men poured through the gates. I would sell one paper to every twentieth man, and sometimes they spoke kindly to me and invited me in to the huge canteen for breakfast, where hundreds of men sat at tables like a scene from Dickens. I loved the breakfasts, black pudding and bubble and squeak, and would have many a cheerful discussion on life and socialism with the men sitting opposite me. They never seemed surprised that a young actress was holding forth to them in their break. I don't know where my confidence came from. After a month, all the teams gathered for a meeting and rehearsal with their different casts, the size of which had expanded beyond our dreams. It was my absolute joy and pride that our Jarrow team had persuaded the local brass band from the colliery to take part, and when they started to play to the assembled hall they were greeted with cheers and tears. We took this collection of plays with actors, miners, railway workers and young people, down to the Empire Pool in Wembley – it was packed out and a resounding success.

It was a unique experience. Nobody ever attempted such an event either before or since, except Danny Boyle, with his inspiring opening to the 2012 Olympics. It made me wonder if he had been in the audience that night at Wembley as a teenager.

There was a dark cloud though. I had persuaded Clive to join the party and it didn't suit him. He was a practical man, and a beautiful and stunning actor. Without him I would now be on the street as he persuaded me to put down money on a small house in Balham. But the harsh and unreasonable demands of the party defeated us – sometimes we only met on sales. We had to spend too much time without each other and we started to argue. We had a deep fondness for one another, so there was no blame on either side, and one day Clive moved out. So I was alone again when, early one December morning at 5.30 a.m., I was woken by a loud knocking.

CHAPTER FIVE

Billingsgate

I
t was Christmas, bazaars were looming. Very crossly and sleepily, I staggered to the door and opened it to Corin, standing there with one of his half-smiles. I didn't see him much these days as he was now on the Central Committee and a full-time organiser.

'I was wondering if you felt like doing Billingsgate this morning.'

'No.' This was unlike me, but I was barely awake and the very thought of the smell of the fish was making me want to throw up. 'No one told me. It was supposed to be tomorrow, not today, and it isn't my turn to go.'

'I know, but you're so famously good at it, and there's no one else. Would you like a coffee?'

He offered me a paper cup of lukewarm coffee he'd had in the car.

There were two fundraising events in the WRP: the Young Socialists' summer and Christmas bazaars. I was elected on to the bazaar committee because of my contacts with the entertainments industry. Also I was very good at asking for money, which was rather shame-making. (At one point I even remember finding myself in the office of Harold Evans, the then editor of *The Sunday Times*, asking for a donation for the paper.) I both hated and loved helping to run these events. The organisation involved was ghastly, but I was terribly good at selling designer clothes on the 'boutique' stall, deriving huge satisfaction from seeing difficult customers go off with a dress that they really liked.

One of the worst jobs, that we all dreaded, was collecting produce from the big markets: Covent Garden for flowers, fruit and veg, or Billingsgate for fish. You had to get there around 5.30–6.00 a.m. and make yourself known to the stall owners, who, depending on their politics, would either send you packing or tell you to come back after the rush. We had to compete with the nuns who were brilliant at begging with charm and authority. If they had got there first you didn't stand a chance. But sometimes we were lucky and got a crate of melons or grapes, and bit by bit we would fill the van with potatoes, cabbages, strawberries – whatever they hadn't been able to sell. I always had to look decent, however early it was; we weren't beggars, asking for charity, but political activists fighting Thatcher, unemployment and racism. Sometimes this was met with a dismissive wave of the hand and a glare – other times a warm coat on the shoulder and a cup of tea. There were Greek and Chinese exporters who could be very generous and I could always tell by the produce that was still there at 7.30 a.m. whether it had been a good morning for them or not.

We were still on the doorstep. I was weakening. 'Look, we'll race round together and it'll be fun.'

In the end I went of course. It was very difficult to stand your ground against Corin if he really wanted you to do something. He went round the big fish stalls collecting dabs, whiting, catfish and many fish I didn't recognise. I did the shellfish, shrimps, cockles, kippers.

Two hours of fish hell in the freezing cold with numb hands from carrying the ice packs and boxes of fish. Both the car and I stank to high heaven. I don't remember what we said on the way back. But I always think that morning was the beginning. Nothing of special significance and yet, as I washed the smell of Billingsgate off my hands in the kitchen sink, I felt as if I'd been on a rather interesting sort of holiday… the kind that you don't want to go home from.

CHAPTER SIX

A Proposal

I t was a sparkling morning in early spring 1976, and the grass was wet with melted frost. The college grounds were rather beautiful, if somewhat neglected. A thrush was singing loudly. Corin was standing, half-leaning, on one side of the gate, and I was on the other. We were enjoying a smoking break in the middle of a lecture at the College of Marxist Education in Derbyshire. The lecture was on The Doctrine of Being from Volume 38 of Lenin's philosophical works on Hegel, and required fierce concentration.

Corin was wearing an old check bomber jacket. He looked good in it. We smoked silently, battling against the habitual fatigue that settled on everyone in the WRP.

Skilfully aiming a cigarette butt into a clump of bushes, Corin said suddenly, 'I've fallen in love with you. Would you like to get married one day?'

A very long pause followed, during which the thrush kept up his singing unaware of the frisson by the gate. Then I replied primly, 'I think you've left it too late Corin, you should have said something before.' I was aware that my heart was beating very fast and despite my pomposity and coolness, I felt very alive.

We returned to the lecture without another word. We had never even kissed, but in writing this I remember we had kissed in a 1970 episode of the television series *Happy Ever After* – as characters – and had got married in a little church. Corin wore a black jacket and pinstriped trousers and I was in a white trouser suit with flares, my hair frothing down my back in curls (it was the Seventies). Far smarter than our actual wedding, in 1985 at Wandsworth Town Hall.

A Proposal

During the filming of *Happy Ever After* we stayed a night in a hotel
in Leeds as we were on location there the next day. We talked and
talked, mostly about politics. I felt rather pleased with myself, because
we got into a political argument about Paris in 1968 that I won. It
was then that I told him about the Socialist Labour League's Friday
night meetings – discussions on Marxism with writers, trade unionists,
teachers, anyone dissatisfied with the slow-drip betrayal of the policies
of the Labour and Communist Parties – and he said he might come.
We also found out that we shared similar experiences, like being sent to
boarding school at too early an age, homesickness, playing the piano,
France, and both having acted with our parents when we were children.
I don't think I thought we could or would have a future together – he
was married and I had a partner – but I felt very much myself with
him, and he made me laugh such a lot. I remember thinking if life had
been different, I might have liked to have ended up with that man.

I agreed to say goodnight to him in his hotel room, which could
have tempted fate and was rather uncharacteristic of me. I opened the
door gingerly to see that Corin was already in bed, and tried not to
notice that he was wearing pale blue poplin pyjamas, old-fashioned and
un-sexy but all the more endearing. We made coffee and tea with the
Teasmade and had shortbread biscuits. It felt like Peter Pan and Wendy.
We said good night and I walked back along the corridor on its blue
and beige flowery carpet. I think I was humming. I wondered whether
he might make it to a Friday night meeting.

CHAPTER SEVEN

New Zealand

After Corin's proposal over the gate we only managed to see each other briefly for the next few weeks, but one day he asked if he could bring his children, Luke and Jemma, down to Lear Cottage for lunch one Sunday. Jemma recently wrote this short memoir about that occasion for *The Sunday Times*:

> I was ten when I first went to Lear Cottage, in the Ashdown forest, East Sussex. My parents, Corin Redgrave and Deirdre Hamilton-Hill, had been separated for three years and, one Saturday, my dad arrived to collect my brother, Luke, and me from our mother's chaotic and bohemian flat in London, to take us away for the week. I was excited, as I thought we were going to visit my grandmother Rachel, but my dad said: "We're going to a comrade's parents."
>
> This didn't go down well. My father was heavily involved with the Workers' Revolutionary Party at the time, so Luke and I assumed this meant another set of dreary rooms with lino floors and clouds of cigarette smoke. Off we set, my heart firmly in my boots, and tipped up at Lear Cottage, so called because of the paintings of Edward Lear that the family owned. It was the home of David Markham and Olive Dehn.
>
> Olive called herself a granarchist and prided herself on not having rules. They had a rescue dog, chickens, some sheep and a couple of pigs. We would be given 10p for a full bucket of weeds and loved nothing better than collecting eggs or taking the pigs for a walk in the forest.
>
> Lear Cottage was small – the Redgraves were forever bumping their heads – and probably built around 1900. It had a porch

over the front door, which nobody ever used, and a red slate roof that came halfway down the house. Through the back door was a little room called the nursery, where there always seemed to be a box of kittens, with cupboards full of toys. Beyond that was the telly room, which was lined with books. In one corner was a ventriloquist's dummy, whose eyes seemed to follow you around. There was also a sitting room with an inglenook fireplace and a piano. My father was a brilliant pianist and would accompany David on his violin.

What we didn't know was that Dad was stepping out with David and Olive's daughter Kika. He waited until the end of the week to say that, if we approved, he would like Kika to be his girlfriend. As we'd had such a brilliant time, we said, "Go for it!" – and Lear Cottage became an important part of our lives.

Until then, I had always been wary of politics – I blamed them for my parents' divorce, and my father was constantly vilified in the press for his views – but through Olive's example, I learnt that politics didn't have to be fuelled by aggression. There was a quieter activism that was all to do with how you led your life and the impact you had on others.

Once we had permission from the children to go out together, things started to get serious. Although their careful chaperoning of us (they came on every walk we went on), it was impossible to find time to be alone. Likewise, in the party, due to the almost inhuman responsibilities placed on comrades, especially Corin, who was now in charge of areas of work such as theoretical articles, building membership, campaigning in Equity, selling papers and so forth. But life itself presented us with a daring plan: to meet on the other side of the world. Corin had been offered the part of Sir George Grey, Governor of New Zealand, in the television series *The Governor,* to be filmed there over some months. And I was due to film *The Blood of Hussein,* in Lahore, Pakistan.

I could fly from Bombay to Wellington and join Corin for the last two weeks of his filming. It was an ambitious plan (there were no mobiles then), and the film crew and I could have been arrested at any time and the film confiscated because it was one of the first 'political' films to be made in Pakistan. In the final week of shooting, I was tempted by a fried carrot and rice dish from a street vendor. I became very, very ill, and was confined to bed in a sort of dormitory in a disused army base in the suburbs of Lahore.

Weak, but determined, I flew from Karachi to Bombay, on to Sydney, then took a small plane to Wellington; but we flew into a terrifying thunderstorm, rocking and bucketing through the air, and, unable to land at Wellington, the plane ended up in Auckland. Eventually all the passengers were steered gently into the airport lounge amongst farmers in shorts and sandals and sounds of sheep and birds that seemed to chime rather than sing. It seemed like a fairy story. We were put up in a little hotel beside the airport, and at 6.00 a.m. we got the plane to Wellington. Only then, from the tiny window, was I able to drink in the beauty of New Zealand – 'Tropical Scotland,' someone remarked. Green hills sloping into white beaches, palm trees and scarlet flowers, but for me, it was the tall jabberwocky trees twisting and hanging over the little chapels and red and white houses that perched on the banks of the frothing Whanganui river that I remember. And the lost piglet on the road that we befriended trying to keep him out of harm's way, and looking for his farm which we never found.

Corin had rented a villa in Days Bay, where the author Katherine Mansfield had lived. All the villas are bungalows and are built on a steep hill. No cars. You go through a little white gate, up stone steps and a steep lane which zigzags to and fro taking you to another little white gate and another bungalow, until you finally reach yours. Each house has a garden competing in intense colours of purple, scarlet, white and yellow flowers with the next, and from ours we could see over the whole bay, over the tops of the dark cedar trees and Surrey-red roofs to the blue ocean, and the ships coming and going. It was just as well that we had landed in Paradise, because I then found the ensuing days very disconcerting.

Going to see Corin on location on the first morning I was transfixed to see him standing, in costume, waist-deep in a wide brown river, embracing a Gauginesque brown-skinned Maori woman whose black hair flowed down her back into the water – and who was naked! The kiss seemed to go on… and on… before the director shouted 'Cut!' and he had to shout it several times before Corin seemed to hear it! Later Corin patiently explained that nothing could be heard above the river and waterfall, that he'd only met her that day and that I must surely know he would never be so unprofessional as to take advantage of her. I was not completely reassured. At the beginning of our courtship Corin had invited me to see him in a show in Manchester, *The Norman Conquests* by Alan Ayckbourn. Corin was very funny, the audience were in stitches, but all I could see was him lying on top of my friend and brilliant actress Margot Leicester and several others in scene after scene. Why oh why did he want me to witness this pornographic orgy? I was gripped by an agonizing and shameful pain: I could not, would not, share him. I suffered from jealousy in all my relationships. Actors, by their nature, are curious, fickle, insecure people; flirts. They should not live together. I would be more suited to a biologist or vet, but as these thoughts raced through my head I already knew I was falling, falling, falling… with no branches to hold on to. No longer were my parents or the WRP the reference points in life. It was him.

Later that evening in Days Bay, as we were unpacking and getting ready to go out to dinner, I saw a handwritten letter in the bottom of his case, with the words 'darling' and 'love' here and there, although I couldn't see properly without picking it up. I was dumbfounded, after all his promises that his womanising days were over I'd caught him out. I stopped talking and started to repack my things.

'Darling what's the matter, what are you doing?'

'Nothing. It's OK, I'm going back to London.'

'WHY?'

'It's obvious you've been in touch, are *still* in touch with some old flame…'

'What on earth are you talking about?'

'I've seen a letter.'

'*What* letter?'

'The one in your case.'

He went and looked and pulled it out. 'This? It's from *you*!'

* * *

We drove around the island exploring, swimming in Lake Taupo, taking a ferry to South Island. Entertaining each other with playing different people and seeing who could be the most fascinating and revolting at the same time. Corin won with Sacha Distel. I was runner-up with Liv Ullmann because I made her too nice. It was the nearest thing to the honeymoon that we never had, and the most romantic two weeks of my life.

A year and a half later I became a mother. A common perception, maybe my own, had seeped down to me that I would be hopeless at motherhood, but it turned out not to be so. Harvey was born on 3 February 1979. I had to have an epidural as the labour was taking too long, and that made the delivery harder as I couldn't feel the muscles to push with. The obstetrician was Iranian and the Iranian Revolution was in full swing. To distract myself from the awful sight of the forceps he was brandishing, I persisted in asking him which side he was on, did he support the revolution, and could he tell me his thoughts about it. I don't remember his answers, but my first beautiful son emerged with a characteristic half-smile on his face.

Arden was born on 2 October 1983 at the South London Women's Hospital. The birth was very fast and there were just three people to help: the midwife, and Jehane and Corin – both of whom I accused of trying to kill me as the pain was so intense and it was too late for drugs.

When the boys were little, I worried that Corin would be forever advising me what to do since he was already an experienced parent. Instead I think I helped him recover from his guilt and sadness about leaving Jemma and Luke when he and Deirdre separated, which often made him cry. Corin moved into my house in Balham, which provided Luke and Jem with not just two new brothers but a second home for them to come to.

Our mainstay during my early years of motherhood was a young woman called Sally Simmons. She had worked and lived with my parents in Sussex and had acquired a unique talent in handling pigs, chickens, children and actors (like my father). She was as brilliant at hearing lines as she was at looking after a three-month-old baby, which was necessary when I had television or film work. She even came to Poland where I was working in the coldest of winters, with both boys. I was the sole breadwinner in those days as Corin had taken the decision only to work if it fitted in with political commitments, which it hardly ever did. Life in the party was extremely hard for couples with children. We were very dependent on Sally, and continue to regard her as a member of our own extended family.

CHAPTER EIGHT

Difficult Times

On 17 December 1983, Dad died of melanoma. The orgone box and Reich totally failed and his illness was painful and terrible, at the end helped only by our kind country GP. My mother was utterly distraught. She gripped the kitchen table, sobbing in anguish as the undertakers climbed the narrow cottage stairs to take him away. My sisters and I tried to unprise her fingers, but she never said goodbye to him.

Clive Merrison, who had a close friendship with Dad, read a letter from Viktor Fainberg, one of my parents' Russian friends, and Corin read from Stanislavski's *My Life in Art* on *An Enemy of the People*. All my partners loved my father, and he them. I am so glad he had been able to hold and admire Arden, who was born two months before he died.

Two years later, Michael Redgrave's Parkinson's disease worsened, and he died on 21 March 1985. The effects of our fathers' deaths bled into our marriage. We were struggling. Corin was still carrying Michael's ashes around in his car, unable to part with them. He didn't want to put Michael into the cold earth. Oh how I understand how he felt now, with Corin so cold in the ground.

I try to comfort myself by remembering Corin never used to feel the cold, at least not as much as I did. I keep some of his ashes on the bookshelf in my bedroom, so a little bit of him will be warm. Of course, anyone who has lost a precious one and has seen them transfigured or transformed into dust knows that one's mind simply cannot grasp the reality of that fact. The transformation of the corporeal into powder, the material, the body of King Lear in a massive fur coat (Corin's), shuffling across the stage, or wearing my father's weather-beaten brown corduroy jacket, driving the car. You look at that powder and some grown-up part of you pretends that you accept that the remains of bone and flesh and wood and clothes and hair and soul can, through intense heat, be ground up into tiny particles and that if you worked at a crematorium you would be entirely at ease with such concepts and sights. I shall never get used to it. Yet I am comforted by the little blue 1940s tin which says in gold lettering, Player's Navy Cut Cigarettes – Gold Leaf – and has a sailor's head, with a ginger moustache, in the middle. I think Corin would have liked it. I wonder where he would have kept me?

Maybe in a coffee cup, or the butter dish.

In the spring of 1985 the WRP waged a campaign to free the sixty-seven miners who had been jailed during the strike. Trade unionists, miners, public health workers, and council leaders marched from Liverpool, Edinburgh and Swansea to attend a packed rally in Alexandra Palace where top-line actors performed a play written by Tom Kempinski and Roger Smith.

On 1 July, the day after this our most successful rally, a letter was read out on the central Committee. The letter accused party leader Gerry Healy of sexual misdemeanours with a number of female comrades. It was the first hammer blow. The next day, on 2 July, the political committee was informed that the party was in debt to the tune of £250,000 and all the cash reserves were exhausted. This was the second blow.

As Alex Mitchell writes in his book *Come the Revolution*, 'Party members with a record of hard-working devotion transformed overnight into… monsters uttering verbal threats as well as physical intimidation'. The party imploded. Healy retired and was only attached to the party as an adviser. But his accusers wanted him expelled, the party shut down. Those of us who wanted to establish the truth through a full inquiry and wanted to keep the party together were called 'rapists'. Corin was locked in a room for several hours and my front window was smashed in by a dustbin which narrowly missed six-year-old Harvey sitting on my lap.

We had to begin again. We raised funds for a new paper, *The Marxist Monthly*. Political revolution was sweeping through Eastern Europe and Russia after the fall of the Berlin Wall. It was the era of *glasnost* (openness) and *perestroika* (reconstruction). We went to Moscow, experiencing the enormous change in the Soviet Union, meeting with members of Memorial, an organization dedicated to the memory of the victims of Stalin. Glasnost meant that archives could at last be opened and read, accounts from the gulags that had never seen the light of day. It was a tremendously exciting time to be in Russia then. Much later, we founded a party that was based on human rights – Peace and Progress, and the Guantanamo Human Rights Commission.

Back in September 1985 I was trying to arrange our wedding, which had been cancelled once owing to the traumatic situation in the party. They weren't fashionable then and I had never even been to one (except in the TV play with Corin). I had no idea what to wear. Luckily, my friend Eluned Hawkins, suggested I ring Shirley Russell the designer. Shirley had made a costume for me in *Clouds of Glory*, Ken Russell's film about Coleridge. She found an elegant black 1940s suit with hat and veil which I liked very much.

We were married on 5 October 1985, an Indian summer's day. My mother made a beautiful spread at the cottage, and we ate outdoors in the autumn sunshine.

'I never thought we'd see the day,' said Jehane, as we were about to drive off.

CHAPTER NINE

1985
Haddock à l'Anglaise

In the first years of being together we both continued to get work as actors, but as our political activities increased we started to be seen as liabilities. Producers were worried that we would hold union meetings during rehearsals, or, even worse, in the lunch hour! That was never the case, but Corin's career suffered through years of blacklisting.

Corin was a natural father and hated being apart from his family. His commitments to the world, which took up so much of his time and energy, were often a source of grievance to all of us.

Holidays were of huge significance and the moment the front door closed he became a different man and totally available to his children. Once, on the first day of a holiday in Ireland, we were just unloading the car when Arden, who was ten at the time and prone to anxieties, asked if he could talk to Corin about some of his worries.

'How many are there?' asked Corin.

'Twenty,' said Arden.

'Righto,' Corin was unfazed.

They sat on the grass and Corin heard every one of them till the dusk came and it was supper time.

'Do you remember that time?' I asked Arden, who is now twenty-nine. 'Yes, very well,' he replied. 'I felt I could ask him anything and he would never be shocked or angry. He was always very comforting.'

Here's an extract from a diary that Corin kept for me as he found himself looking after the boys on holiday in Italy without me when I got a job unexpectedly. I should explain that when we went on holiday Corin and I pretended to be a couple of rich North Americans who

were always trying to buy up castles or villas. They were called Ethel
and Hiram.

Corin's diary for Kika

Sunday, 19 August 1987

Lunigiana, Italy

A week ago, so 'Tim' (our landlord) told us at Castagneto
(Aston Villa), an awesome thunderstorm crashed over the
Lunigiana valleys, and since then the air has been sweeter and
cooler. Certainly the night air in Campocontro is cool. My
bedroom window is open. It is 5.15 a.m. and I'm waiting for
the dawn.

A mad (or ghostly?) huntsman has been blazing away with
his shotgun all night long in our valley. He seems to be
particularly active now, letting off a cartridge every thirty
seconds or so. Our neighbour's dog sounds very like Kika's
imitation of a dog. He is also an insomniac, and barks every
half an hour through the night.

Campocontro scores 9 out of 10 for the friendliness of its
inhabitants, who all smiled and returned our 'buonasera'
with a very passable show of warmth: 10 out of 10 for
picturesqueness: but for tranquility I'm afraid, it is doubtful
if it can even score 1 out of 10. Hiram, of course, snored
peacefully through every explosion, at least until 4.45 a.m.

But, of course, he had four glasses of wine at La Galeta last night from the very large carafe on his table, and was about to have six more, when he remembered that he had two boys to drive home, not to speak of Ethel and himself. Ethel, on the other hand, I'm sorry to say, despite bunging her ears full of wax and placing a sleeping mask over her eyes, did not sleep a wink, what with the dog and the mad huntsman. She is not too keen on the bats either, which flit to and fro outside her bedroom window.

La Galeta was just like old times, very friendly barman and sweet waitress. The boys had ravioli con ragu and lamb. After supper we played three games of table-top football. The blue player has a distinct advantage because the table slopes so that the ball rolls into the red goal mouth. Harvey beat the combined team of Arden and Corin, two games to one, though Arden did manage some spectacular saves. He is the Bruce Grobbelaar of pin table football, saving the almost impossible shots, and letting in the easy ones.

6.00 a.m.

Dawn at last. And a chorus of birds, singing so rarely (Walter Scott) and sweetly. And the church bell in Amola, our nearest village. And the cockerels. And still the mad huntsman blazes away, and now I think he's been joined by his brother in the next valley. I wish I had a tape recorder – no city dweller could imagine how NOISY the countryside can be at this hour of day. Balham is silent by comparison.

7.20 a.m.

The sun has risen above the tree tops. Sunshine is streaming into my bedroom window. A beautiful second awakening. Harvey is a wonderful companion. Very funny and observant, and a great help at reading road signs.

Day 1 (Sunday) – On the beach at San Terenzo

Arden spends all morning in the water, swimming, diving, and splashing about in the dinghy. Before we set off he said 'I'm starting to miss Mummy.' San Terenzo is very, very crowded. But the sea is lovely, just the right temperature. Lunch at Great Feelings which is very nice, despite its name. Then back on the beach until 2.30. We're very short of cash now, only 24,000 lire to last the rest of the day, and I'm trying to figure out how we are going to telephone you (and V) and have dinner.

With only 24,000 lire in our pockets, it's clear that CR is going to have to cook dinner. So off to Licciana Nardi, where no shops are open. On to Crespiano. We devise a very complicated, scabrous game, which goes like this: the first person to see an open shop will never be a bumhole for the rest of his life. The other two will not automatically be condemned to everlasting bumholishness, they will merely remain potential bumholes. This gives everyone hope, and we all look eagerly for an open shop, and find one, simultaneously, in Cuspiano. We spend 15,400 lire. 2,300 lire on the phone call. 1,000 lire on games. Not bad.

The meal, back home, is rather good, and makes me quite ambitious to cook more. Only it is marred by an awful accident, so heartrending I cannot bring myself to write about it.

[I never found out what it was; KM]

We manage to get Arden to bed, then C and Harvey talk for half an hour about (a) missing Kika, (b) the problems of life, and (c) the pros and cons of optimism and pessimism.

Whenever we got the chance, Corin and I arranged to go to our little Montparnasse studio flat that we rented in Paris through Suzanne Schiffman. Rue Boulard runs at right angles to Rue Daguerre and along the tip of Montparnasse Cemetery, where celebrities like Gainsbourg, Sartre, de Beauvoir and Beckett are buried. Our flat, no. 17 Rue Boulard, was above a Vietnamese hairdresser and next door to the famous restaurant – Au Vin des Rues. An establishment run by a terrifying and jovial patron with a black handlebar moustache. His food was not for wimps. His speciality was all kinds of meat, and the helpings were enormous; trotters, tripe, steak, venison. He kept a roving watch on all his customers and eyed you with great disfavour if you were having difficulty finishing your meal. Jehane and I were caught trying to tip our food into my handbag, so we could never go back.

Opposite was a café where we often had breakfast. A bittersweet experience because although we'd been coming there for a good four years, the barman or owner never greeted us, or worse, even remembered us. And despite ingratiating ourselves to a humiliating extreme, we never got a smile out of him. More galling was the fact that we saw him laughing and joking with other customers. Did he hate us because we were English? Or did he just not give a damn and had a short-term memory problem? We fantasised about how we could make him acknowledge us but it never happened.

The flat was one room with a bedroom and bathroom off it. We had a table by the windows overlooking the street, and a leather armchair and a tiny fridge for paté, melon and wine. When we got off the Metro (line 4) at Denfert-Rochereau and walked through the market, passing the stalls of crabs and lobsters, strawberries, melons, and wine, I would stop at the florists to buy a bunch of spring flowers and Corin would pick up a bottle of wine – oh happy, happy days! (Though at the time I was always yearning for the 'perfect' flat with a garden.)

The flat represented the most extravagant, impossible, but wonderful dream that we had denied ourselves during our most puritanical days in the Workers' Revolutionary Party. It was there that we found some extra valuable time for each other and the boys, who loved to come despite the cramped conditions. We could resume the long-running stories of our childhoods, something we were always fascinated by; our different backgrounds. We made unrealistic plans for the future and reassessed the old wounds we had inflicted on one another. One way of doing this was to write a story about some minor incident from the other's point of view, exposing a deadly (and we thought witty) insight into one another. It was a way of getting revenge while laughing about it. Here are two such stories.

Haddock à l'Anglaise
by Kika Markham

The café they had chosen was closed for Sunday, so they found a rather traditional American Left Bank sort of place.

They were shown to their seats by an elegant but tiny head waiter. She chose coquilles Saint-Jacques à la Normande and he ordered haddock à l'Anglaise.

'But darling, why choose that in Paris?'

He weakened and changed his order to saumon avec pommes purée. They forgot that he had changed his order and brought him the haddock anyway. The house wine was particularly good and his wife, most uncharacteristically, could not fault it. He was a little preoccupied. Thinking about Monday's rehearsal and whether to invite the leading actress to lunch and allow a little more 'adventure' into the proceedings. His wife was attempting to ask the waiter something in very bad French and he tactfully explained the right phrasing. Poor love, she certainly needs those classes but I must be careful not to parade my knowledge too readily. She gets very defensive, he thought.

He was just giving an extremely good example of perfect syntactical French when suddenly the room went dark and he couldn't breathe. He was choking horribly and tears poured into his eyes. She was looking at him quizzically.

'Do you want a slap on the back?'

He couldn't nod, let alone speak. Coughs wrenched him. His lungs weren't getting any air. He waggled his fingers feebly.

'Does that mean no?'

Again that curiously detached little smile and a small pucker of worried frown but then she started to eat again. He wiped the tears from his cheeks, still unable to breathe or speak. She probably wouldn't be able to call for an ambulance with her French. He was going to die in Paris in a minicab with her sympathetically watching him vomit into a plastic bag.

He heard himself wheezing, as if far away, and the room began to come back into focus. No one was running to the table or even looking concerned, except his wife.

'Oh darling, that was awful,' she said, 'I wanted to slap your back but you seemed to say "No".'

'I couldn't breathe,' he said. 'Was it a bone?'

'I don't know what it was. Something stuck. My mouth was too full.'

'I was really frightened. I had visions of... well...'

She didn't finish.

'Yes, so did I for a moment,' he said, 'but fortunately the choking subsided and I realised I was going to live.'

She hesitated and he knew she was wrestling with herself.

'Don't whatever you do, say: "It was a pity you chose the haddock".'

'No.' She paused. 'We'll just say it was an unfortunate mistake.'

He sighed. Had he got anything in common with this mongrel woman? God knows how their marriage had lasted so long. She was looking at him, radiantly sorrowful, hiding a smirk behind her napkin.

'Truly darling, I'm not trying to score points. We've had such a lovely holiday and the last thing I want is that this incident becomes…' she paused, blushing, and he couldn't help being touched in spite of himself, '…becomes a bone of contention between us. Whoops. Sorry.'

Only Choking
by Corin Redgrave

'I don't see why,' she said, 'Why is it worse for William?'

'Because William didn't choose to leave his children.'

William and William's misery had been their topic of conversation for the past hour. Subjects like these, the problems of their married friends, helped to disguise their own. But sometimes, as now, they helped to expose the fundamental fault lines of their own relationship.

'I don't think you understand the problem,' he was saying, 'It's not your fault, it's no lack of sympathy on your part. You can't understand it because you haven't experienced it. I have, you see.'

'That's the South African argument.'

'The what?'

'Before Mandela. When a white racist from South Africa couldn't convince one of the natural justice of apartheid, he'd end up saying you couldn't understand it because you hadn't been there.'

'Excusez-moi!' she signalled to a waiter, 'Je veux change.'

Her vocabulary was small and her grammar, non-existent, but her accent was so convincing and she spoke so confidently that she managed to make herself understood. For her husband it was maddening, this ease with which she managed to communicate in mangled French. Whereas he who had been educated to speak fluently, with flawless grammar, must struggle to make himself understood.

And even then would end up being served with what he hadn't ordered.

'Do you mind if I correct you?' he asked warily, evenly, 'I wouldn't normally...'

'Oh yes you would, you love correcting me.'

'No, not as a rule. Only I thought, as you're taking French lessons, it might be helpful.'

'Most helpful,' she said, gritting her teeth, 'What did I get wrong?'

'Changer. It's an infinitive.'

'That's what I said.'

'No, you said, 'Je veux change,' which is meaningless.'

'He seemed to understand.'

'Of course. He understood your intention.'

Silence. Her husband sighed, feeling misunderstood. And then, embarrassed by the silence, began to speak of William again. His publisher. Poor misunderstood William who hadn't chosen to leave his children.

She let him talk. He had a nice melodious voice, not too loud. She used to tell him that his voice was one of the things that had made her fall in love with him. And newspaper interviewers, even if they could find nothing else particularly flattering to say about him, would always remark on his voice, and how he managed to talk for minutes on end in unbroken sentences of perfect syntax.

Only lately, she had found she wasn't listening any more. She preferred to cut off, think her thoughts, and let him talk on, like the water in a babbling brook, forcing its way over stones worn smooth by its flow, through cracks widened by its pressure.

'What were you thinking?' he asked. He had been talking uninterrupted for some minutes. She had been thinking about his deviousness. How he liked to hold everything apart, couldn't bear the prospect of monogamy, had to encourage other women that they, but for the grace of God – 'I was thinking how strange. That your cock had to keep stuffing itself in all those holes. And how odd for so many holes, to have so many cocks stuffed in them.'

A woman at the next table, plump and with bubbly, frizzy hair, turned and smiled, raising her glass. Silence. He liked such remarks in private, often encouraged her to talk dirty, but froze with embarrassment that they'd been overheard.

But soon he was talking again. She smiled and nodded, and thought her own thoughts. How nice, she thought, to be like the couple at the next table, who hadn't said a word for ten minutes, but seemed perfectly happy in one another's company. German, or perhaps Dutch. They smiled at one another, and twice she had seen the young woman stroking her boyfriend's knee under the table.

Suddenly she became aware that her husband was waving at her, and that his face was red, almost purple. His eyes were streaming with tears and he was coughing as if trying to clear his throat.

'Quick darling, eat some bread,' she said and called for some water. 'Was it a bone?'

He had been eating haddock à l'Anglaise, which was maddening of him, in a French restaurant. He kept waving his hand, like a paw, to and fro, as if trying to reassure her. For a split second, she was aware of the power of life or death over him. That would be the perfect murder, wouldn't it? Or rather manslaughter? Or was it even manslaughter, a *crime passionnel*, if you simply let your husband die for boring you to death, correcting you till you could scream with frustrated anguish.

Would it be manslaughter if I let him choke on his fishbone, fall face forward into his haddock à l'Anglaise?

'Better?' she said, thumping him vigorously, and not without a certain malevolence, bruisingly between the shoulders, 'Feeling any better now?'

He was gasping, wiping his eyes.

'Yes, thanks, only you shouldn't hit someone like that if they're choking. Read any first aid book. It's an old wives' tale that that's what you should do.'

'Thanks,' she said. 'Thanks for correcting me!'

CHAPTER TEN

1993
Moving Theatre

It wasn't until the Nineties that Corin started to be employed as an actor again, thanks entirely to Annie Castledine and David Thacker: *Rosmersholm* and *Measure for Measure* at the Young Vic. He would remember their support for the rest of his life. The deaths of our fathers and continual worry over money made us fragile. We felt estranged from one another and felt the need to work together again once more, something we had not done since the beginning of our relationship. This led to the formation of the Moving Theatre company in 1993. Our first play was *The Flag* (adapted by Alex Ferguson from a novel by Robert Shaw), which Corin directed and we were both in. Our friend Donald Sartaine was at the helm and our sons sold programmes after school at the tiny theatre in Bridge Lane, Battersea.

Our second season was at the Riverside Studios, where Vanessa and Rade Šerbedžija acted memorably in *The Liberation of Skopje*, a well-known Yugoslavian classic. No one could forget the scene where they were chopping cabbage at a table and were interrupted by a rider on a beautiful white horse – which resided, for performances, on the riverside terrace outside the theatre. Arden, aged nine, joined the company, playing a refugee. Corin directed me in *Real Writing*, a play by Maureen Lawrence about Akhmatova and her struggle to save her poetry under Stalin. Malcolm Tierney was brilliant in Frisch's *The Fire Raisers*, and the programme also included a play by Alex Ferguson about Roger Casement. This ambitious season all but bankrupted us and we remortgaged our house, which I'm still paying for today, but in those days we didn't look ahead. In 1994 we produced five monologues. Corin adapted Oscar Wilde's 'De Profundis', the letter from Reading Gaol to his lover Lord Alfred Douglas. I had written to Tony Kushner asking him if he could write a short piece for me. I had in mind something ten minutes long that he'd possibly had in a drawer. We were friends and had kept in touch for some years, as I'd been in his wonderful play, *A Bright Room Called Day*, at the Bush Theatre. But the piece he wrote wasn't short: it was an extraordinary, poetic, hour-long meditation on Afghanistan, loneliness, war and love.

Tony arrived with the script of *Homebody/Kabul* two days before I was due to perform it, so I had to do a rehearsed reading, directed by Annie Castledine. Later on it took three months to learn for its world premiere at the Chelsea Centre directed by David Esbjornson. I was helped by Sally Simmons in the garden who copied Corin's method of learning, i.e. to do it out of doors (all Corin's lines were learned striding over Tooting Common). I am embarrassed to write that I rang Tony several times to plead with him to make it shorter and (worse) to ask if I could do the seventy-minute monologue in a Scots, American, or Northern accent as using a dialect seemed to give me confidence. All these requests were ignored until finally Tony rang from Canada with the reply: 'Homebody has never travelled, she is London-based – I heard your voice when I wrote it, you are frightened of committing to the role nakedly. You don't need these props...'

On the opening night my nerves were both agonising and paralysing. Not for the first time, Corin saved me. But I had to use his 'infallible method' – made up on the spur of the moment – which meant being held upside down for several minutes. He convinced me to stand on my head in the dressing room while he held my ankles. It worked.

On 15 July Tony faxed me:

Dearest Kika,

Thank you for asking me to write this play and thank you for inspiring it. I'm very proud of it and very proud of you – I know this hasn't been an easy journey for you, but you've been valiant and brave and I have absolute confidence that the performance is as wonderful as my spies… are telling me it is.

Tony

Later Tony wrote Act Two and it became a full-length play. The UK premiere in 2002 was at the Young Vic in a Cheek by Jowl production directed by Declan Donnellan.

In 1999 Corin took his adaptation of 'De Profundis', first performed in the Moving Theatre company season, to New York. The distinguished theatre critic Clive Barnes wrote an enthusiastic review:

Finally, a brief note on Corin Redgrave's one-man show at a one-night Actor's Fund Benefit, last Sunday at Circle in the Square. It was a magnificent virtuoso performance of Oscar Wilde's "De Profundis".

Redgrave is, very simply, a great actor. Except for cultivating the faintest Irish brogue, he didn't try to portray Wilde – yet his performance had the magic transparency of truth.

New York Post, 23 May 1999

In November 2000 Corin brought it to the National Theatre in London. In *The Independent*, critic Paul Taylor praised Corin's 'wonderful performance':

He pours out thought and feeling with just the right manic edge of someone who has spent too much time alone and has begun to talk to absent people as if they were really there. While you were watching and listening to it, this is a performance that lies too deep for tears. It was the next day that it made me break down.

The family came together for *A Song at Twilight* by Noël Coward. Vanessa, Corin, me, and Mathew Bose. Bill Kenwright produced, and Sheridan Morley directed for the first time. Rehearsals were not peaceful. Vanessa and Corin argued a lot. Vanessa as the elder felt she knew more, but Corin as the younger always wanted to have the last word. As for me, I sometimes felt paralysed by Vanessa's fearlessness.

My scenes were mostly with Corin. I played Hilde, his put-upon wife and secretary. The mixture of irritation and fondness was great fun too; the crosser Corin became, the more the audience enjoyed it.

Corin wrote of Michael Redgrave's Crocker-Harris in *The Browning Version* that there was no safety net under his performance. Feeling safe on stage was an unknown experience for me but there *was* a safety net when I worked with Corin because he was so very at home on stage himself. Having said this, it was not always an easy ride working with him. When I told Stephen Frears that Corin and I were going to work together, he said, 'You'd better get a good lawyer.' Of course, we've had bitter arguments. We were doing lines for *The Country Girl* at Greenwich, directed by Annie Castledine, and Corin was ticking me off, saying: 'That's not what Clifford Odets wrote. Stick to the line.' Then I was hearing *his* lines – and one was totally different. But he said, 'No, no, I think Odets is wrong here. It's better like this. For you it's better to stick to the text, but for me it isn't.' *Outrageous.*

At the end of *A Song at Twilight*, Hilde comes back drunk and explains to Hugo and Carlotta (Corin and Vanessa) in a heart-stopping speech what it was like to be a German after the war. One of the few times in my life I talked for four minutes to my husband and sister-in-law without being interrupted. The play was a huge success and ran in the West End for several months. Our mothers came to see us and sat in a box, blowing kisses at the curtain calls.

Corin sent me a letter about another family episode, when he and Vanessa took their mother, Rachel, to Venice:

> Torcello is a small island, criss-crossed with canals like a miniature version of its grander patron Venice, but very green, covered in trees, bushes, wild grasses and poppies. There are houses instead of palaces, and even the Cipriani which is famous and expensive is quite relaxed and homely in appearance. We were recommended to the Osteria al Ponte del Diavolo by Tasha and Liam. It was much less expensive and even more unassuming in appearance. The restaurant garden was very beautiful with a meadow in front, and a long line of linden trees. Rachel grumbled a little that it wasn't the Cipriani, and took some convincing that even Tasha and Liam thought it nicer. But it certainly was. A lovely simple lunch. Tagliatelli ai piselli, and fritto misto di mare. All the time I wish you were there, wondering what you would think of this and that…

> After lunch we went into the church. Late medieval, and therefore quite austere by comparison with Venice's renaissance churches and cathedrals. Very fine, but the remains of the martyrs, embalmed in glass-sided catafalques, little shrivelled sacred monsters. Despite all its immense beauty and splendour there is something truly repulsive about Catholic Christianity's worship of death…

> R is becoming more difficult: or rather, the periods when she is her old sweet jolly self have become much shorter, and her periods of fretting over the most inconsequential, unnecessary worries have become correspondingly longer. They are always hydra-headed, so that the moment you succeed in allaying one worry, up pops another to take its place:

> (after I have just bought a tablecloth for you)

> V: Isn't it lovely Mama?

R: Yes. But what can I buy? I so wanted to get a present for Corin, and of course I should get one for Kika.

V: What would you like to buy?

R: Corin says he doesn't want anything. Not even a tie?

V: Corin doesn't wear ties.

R: He used to. So he doesn't want anything? Nothing at all?

C: *(An inspiration.)* You could buy me a cake.

R: A cake? What sort of a cake?

V: There are lots of lovely little patisseries in the alleyways near the hotel…

R: But will I have enough money?

V: Oh yes, heaps, they really aren't expensive.

R: Very well. If you say so. I'll get Corin a cake. Which means getting up at dawn I suppose?

V: No, there's no hurry at all.

R: Yes, but I've got to buy a cake.

C: *(Slightly acerbic.)* Get up at one o'clock, as usual. That gives you two hours before lunch to buy a cake.

R: So I've got to spend the whole morning shopping for a cake.

C: It'll probably take you five minutes.

R: What size of cake?

C: Average.

R: *(To V.)* What does he mean, *average*?

I often thought that Corin was only really, truly happy when he was working with members of his family. He had acted as a child with Rachel at Stratford and in his *Guardian* article on playing Lear he said: 'My father was leading the Memorial Theatre Company, playing Shylock, Antony and Lear. My mother played Regan. I learned to love the sound of Shakespeare from my father but it was she who taught me to love Shakespeare's stories. It had never occurred to me to read *King Lear* before seeing it. I simply asked my mother to tell me the story'. And later he played Coriolanus at the Young Vic with Rachel as Volumnia, my friend Geraldine Griffiths as Virgilia, and Harvey as Young Martius.

This was a very enjoyable experience for all three, only marred by Rachel rather too often coming in over Harvey's only line:

A' shall not tread on me;
I'll run away until I am bigger, but then I'll fight.

It was difficult not to be cross with one's grandmother in such circumstances, especially so if his school friends happened to be at the performance. Sometimes Harvey would cry with rage to Corin on their way home. However, this was the year of the beginning of a life-long love affair with Arsenal. After his scene Harvey would run backstage to watch football on the stage manager's TV, and that year, to his joy and amazement, he saw them win the league! His one and only professional acting job (so far) is thus forever associated with Arsenal's victory. This Arsenal addiction has affected the whole family, none more so than Corin.

Kate Stokes, who worked with him at the RSC, sent me this short anecdote:

I met Corin in January 2005, when he played King Lear in the Albery Theatre RSC season. I was part of the stage crew. I was only really on nodding terms with any of the cast, but then somebody told me that Corin was a 'gooner' (an Arsenal fan for the uninitiated), so, quite timidly, I approached him in the wings one night and asked him if this was true. I explained that we were the only two gooners in a theatre full of rabid Manchester United fans, which he found quite amusing. There was a point in the show where we would both be in the stage-left wing for a few minutes, me in my set-shifting outfit, Corin in full 'blasted heath' regalia; a massive coat made of fur scraps, with two prop hares slung around his neck, and we would talk, naturally enough, about Arsenal. I remember thinking 'I'm chatting to King Lear about why we can never beat Bolton'. It doesn't get any better than this!

In 1998 Vanessa had discovered a little-known Tennessee Williams play, *Not About Nightingales*, and took it to Trevor Nunn who directed it. It is a dark, passionate play about the penal system in the US, and it had a terrific part for Corin: Boss Whalen. It was the first time Corin had worked with Trevor Nunn since *Julius Caesar* at the RSC in 1972 and it had huge emotional significance for him. He felt he'd come back in from the cold. It opened at the National Theatre and transferred to Broadway, where Corin won several awards for his performance.

Corin had found Kathy and Henry Chalfant through Tony Kushner and was happily living in their house in Greenwich Village. Kathy had been in Tony's play *Angels in America*, and had won the Drama Desk Award for her unforgettable performance in *Wit* by Margaret Edson. She shared the house with Henry's cousin Charles Ramsburg, a painter, and Michele Zackheim, a painter and writer. It was a bright house with tall windows, dark polished floors, comfortable sofas, and paintings everywhere. There were always actors or writers dropping by, and lots of theatre gossip and political discussion. I was able to visit him a couple of times; living there together was one of the happiest times in our lives. It remains our second home to this day.

This is an extract from Corin's New York diary, which he kept while I was in London:

Tuesday 9 February 1999

Day 10

It's an age since I wrote this diary. All my good intentions to write it at least every other day have been sabotaged by the unusually heavy workload of writing for the magazine [*The Marxist*].

It's the second very long day of technical rehearsal. I have a nice spacious dressing room, with a shower and loo. When I get the chance I'll get a divan brought in, and a fridge, and put some of our beautiful photos on the wall. They made me cry with joy, and a little bit with pain, because they make you seem so close and yet you're so far. At night I play your "I'm beginning to miss you", and I could swear you must be thinking of me, except I know – or I hope – you're asleep.

My dresser, Dino, has been dressing Uta Hagen. She's on in a play off-B'way, which will run for another three weeks. Another good reason you should hurry on over if humanly possible, to catch her while she's still here. Dino says she's a 'miracle' and I'm sure he's right.

Wednesday 10 February 1999
Postscript – Morning of 11th day

Lynn rang this morning. She's coming to the theatre in
our dinner break, between 6.00 p.m. and 7.30, so I'll learn
more. Then Vanessa. She confessed to feeling depressed and
terribly stressed. I said she must take a holiday, in March, and
I offered to look after Rachel in New York from March 7th
approx, until March 24th, when you come out. I may live to
regret this. And, finally, just before I left the apartment, Tasha
rang (!!!). She's just been speaking to Lynn, and now she's
coming with Lynn, to my first preview, this Saturday (!!!)

When I returned to New York in March I noticed Corin was more tired
than usual. He had had a terrible fall backstage and nearly broken his
nose. Also, he was having to pee with worrying frequency. But it wasn't
until autumn, just before the rehearsals for *The Cherry Orchard* at the
National Theatre began, that he agreed to go for a check-up with our
doctor. This led to a hospital referral and a biopsy. Corin kept a diary:

Roger Kirby Clinic Autumn 2000

There's nowhere to sit, so we stand, Kika and I, holding
hands. Sylvia whispers that Mr Kirby will see us early, i.e. he'll
leap-frog us over other patients who have been waiting longer.
I don't expect and I don't really want preferential treatment,
and certainly don't deserve it. Sure enough after a very few

minutes more Kirby emerges from his office and calls out my name. We go through dates. He says that I shouldn't wait till the end of March when *The Cherry Orchard* is over, I should have the operation at the earliest possible date.

I don't feel as sad as I thought I would about leaving *The Cherry Orchard* early. That will come, no doubt. But it's as though another age of innocence has ended. The first age came to an end when Kirby told me I had prostate cancer, and Kika and I walked hand in hand, slightly in shock, through the corridors of St George's, trying to digest the fact that we had crossed a rubicon from good health, well fairly good health, to a very definite kind of disorder. Illness? I can't yet think of it as illness, because I don't feel ill.

The second age, half-innocent, half-knowing, came here, in Kirby's consulting room.

Thursday/Friday 2 and 3 January, 2001

My second immersion in the tube, the magnetic resonance image maker. The same clicking and clacking, like those big wooden rattles which used to frighten horses, but this time the clattering persisted, on and on, for minutes on end. The thought crossed my terrified mind that the machine had got stuck at a certain phase of its programme.

And since there was an intercom voice to reassure me, I pictured the technicians wrestling helplessly to bring the machine back into control, while I suffocated inside. The investigation took about three quarters of an hour, far longer than before, and that was nerve-wracking too.

What was it looking for and why was it taking so long? When I was finally released I said, in that feeble jocular mock-complaining tone one hopes will prompt explanations, "Well, that took a long time." But the technician simply said, "Oh dear, did it?"

The next day the waiting room was fuller than ever before, and all the old men and their wives (old men? It's like those villages in Provence where every English person except oneself is a 'tourist'). We're sitting in rows of fixed seating, at right angles to each other, so the only thing to look at was one's neighbour's gloomy profile. Sylvia, Roger Kirby's secretary, introduces herself, blonde, middle-aged, attractive. If I were Alan Clark (d. 1999, aged 71, of cancer) I'd chat her up. Instead I ask her an inane question about Christmas, "Did you get drunk?" And then followed up by offering her tickets for *The Cherry Orchard*. I can only hope she put it down to nervousness.

Kirby asks us if we had a good Christmas. An ominous beginning. I've learned to expect that, when the appointment begins with small talk, there is bad news coming. They're "a little worried" about a lymph node which shows up enlarged on the scan. A warning that I shouldn't delay any more. All my carefully built defences begin to crumble. I had banked on the tumour being so small and slow-growing that I could finish *The Cherry Orchard*, say farewell to the cast and quietly exit into hospital.

Roger Kirby was unable to operate on Corin as there was a hernia obstructing the route, so we had to fight the cancer through radiotherapy and drugs. We were treated brilliantly by Roz Eyles at the Royal Marsden Hospital, and Corin would look forward to going as we sometimes met our friends Jim MacKeith or Harold Pinter at Le Colombier, a very chic restaurant opposite.

A year and a half later, when Corin's treatment was finished – and in a break from rehearsing *No Man's Land* (directed by Pinter himself) – we went to Sweden for a little holiday for Corin to recuperate from the radiotherapy. I wrote a short story about it.

Mauvais Goût (Bad Taste) May 2003

The sunlight forced his eyes open. He'd had another bad dream about Pinter scolding him and him not being able to explain why he had chosen a particular gesture.

He got up for a pee, a wearisome activity, although of late, a little easier. He was in the recovery period from radiotherapy, but the improvement felt slow. He noticed his wife's bed – empty – the duvet in a tossed heap of fury. Perhaps she's gone for a walk. He looked at his watch. 4.00 a.m. Christ! The room was bathed in light, burning through the flimsy cotton curtains. They were in Sweden, where the sun came up at

3.30, for five days to recuperate from the radiotherapy. It was needed after the trauma of not just having cancer, but the after effects of the so-called "cure". Not that he wasn't optimistic – he was. He believed in the doctor's positive prognosis. It didn't keep him awake at night. And even if he felt the presence of gloomy, even morbid thoughts, he was able to divert them before they struck with full force, and drift into sleep with images of country lanes, actresses he had worked with, his children, sandy beaches, his father, the book that he'd written about his father, and finally his last two stage performances. Not so his wife. He didn't even bother to ask how she's slept because he knew the answer. Oh the punishment inflicted on those who sleep by those who don't. To fall asleep was a skill he'd learnt since childhood, but however he'd tried, had failed to pass it on to her.

He rarely complained, but sometimes a sharp stabbing pain, low down, made him gasp and immediately she would turn a worried frown toward him, "What's wrong?" And he'd have to reassure her. As he did with his mother and his sisters. It seemed that he was forever doomed to be resolutely cheerful, brave, paternal, fraternal – even light-hearted about his own illness.

His wife's constant worrying was exhausting for both of them. Anyway, here they were in Sweden on Midsummer's Eve, June 21st. The sky was bulging with black clouds. The fjord in front of their cottage window was an expanse of white with a dull skyline of brown rock and scrub. Little more than a third-rate Scottish loch. Nothing moved outside and now it was raining. They'd eaten Swedish meatballs (frozen) and baked potato for lunch and she was attempting to hang out some washing on the wet clothes line. He was staring at his text in the pretence of learning but inwardly seething with pain and anger.

Turning over her notebook he'd read something she'd written about him. It wasn't complimentary. A close friend of theirs,

Suzanne Schiffman, had died two weeks ago – his wife had been in Paris for the funeral. *The Independent* wanted a personal memoir, and as he couldn't locate her he thought he should do the next best thing and write some words in the spirit that she would like. He had had to read it over the telephone and, typically, she had objected to several things about it (typically because, of course, she hadn't got around to or wasn't capable of writing it herself!). Only she could turn something that he'd done, out of a genuine wish to help, into something rather cheap and even "sensation seeking" making him feel dirty and dishonourable. She did it with such a deft sleight of hand – like flouring a fish before carefully putting it in the frying pan. Later on, she re-read the piece, and gave it her approval and apologized. But now the wound had opened again seeing the words, "…it was good copy [for him] to write about me and an ex-lover, unnecessary for an obituary, mauvais gout!" and a whole lot more in the notebook about how unfair it was that he would once more, using the famous family name, obliterate her with his own elegant style of writing, seizing that chance yet again to see his name in print. "It's made me quite upset." He started rather quietly.

"What has?" Her voice shot up in a querulous, over-defensive way, so familiar to him.

"The way you describe me as 'my dear husband'…and 'such good copy'…'mauvais gout'… As if you see me through a telescope or a mirror." He meant, as if you've stopped loving me.

"I told you at the time I didn't like what you wrote."

"How would you feel if I referred to you as 'my dear wife'?"

"Look," she said. "You know I get quite jealous of you – that you're much more articulate and fluent than me. And what's more you even get asked to write about things that can only concern me. I get resentful." A subject she never tired of, his famous family, his career, his education and the lack of hers. He went upstairs and put his hands over his face. She thought that maybe he was crying. He had been wiping his glasses but it could have been the steam of the baked potato. Lying on his back he was asleep in two minutes.

Later, as a small chink of blue appeared, they went for a walk to see if they could meet – well – their neighbours or even just a friendly person who might invite them to their house for a midsummer drink. They had made friends again but felt horribly lonely and excluded from the festivities. And a sadness was between them.

At the end of the lane they saw a garden full of people. They were sitting at a long table with little children playing nearby. There was a huge maypole covered with branches, leaves and flowers and ribbons. A very large seagull or albatross stood on a chimney overseeing the proceedings. It was an enchanting sight. "I'd love to take a photo of them," she sighed. "Go on then, they won't mind."

"Oh no, we can't. We shouldn't be going past their garden anyway – it looks pathetic, so intrusive..." As she spoke, a friendly woman waved to them from the table.

"There you are. They don't mind at all." He took a photograph of them and she smiled once more. They walked on round the corner. "You know it was you that told me to write down what I was feeling in the first place, and so I did." She decided not to risk any more. "I've got over it now." He smiled magnanimously.

They walked back past the blue lupins and yellow buttercups, sounds of the midsummer party receding like an offstage recording in a Chekhov play. At home they opened their first bottle of schnapps. "It's when it reaches here that you can taste it." He touched his chest…

2004
Perugia

In May 2004 Corin and I went on holiday, to stay with Michele and Charlie in Tuscany. After a quiet week, Corin and I decided to go to Perugia for a night, to see the jazz festival and have a romantic supper in a taverna.

Perugia is built on hills. You have to park your car at the bottom and walk to the top. We were both breathless when we reached the beautiful old square but I remember we had a pleasant meal and that Corin seemed to be fine. On the way back, though, he said he didn't feel up to going to the concert and we should go to our hotel instead. This meant climbing some more and I could see that he was beginning to feel really bad. By the time we found our hotel he was shivering and shaking like a leaf – I could tell he had a high fever and was also talking nonsense very rapidly, which was most alarming. I got the hotel receptionist to call a doctor, fearing that on a Saturday night with a jazz festival in town we'd never get one, but this being Italy they found Dr Mario, who promised to come soon.

Never had two hours gone so slowly. Eventually the doctor arrived and examined Corin, who seemed to have reached a peak and was starting to pour with sweat. Dr Mario was elegant with beautifully kept white hair. He looked kind but grave. He explained in his excellent English that he couldn't tell if it was very bad flu or whether it might have been a heart attack. And then he said (and I never forgot his manner, words or how he said them), 'You must watch him, keep a good eye on him, signora, and get his heart looked at when you return home.' He gave me a pill to put under Corin's tongue if he felt ill. He also gave me a prescription. 'You will find a pharmacist open, even at this time of night.'

I ran up the hill against the streams of people singing and shouting. The beautiful piazza was teeming with life and a jazz band was playing on stage. I didn't hear it, I was trying to find the chemist but there seemed to be nobody that knew the town – they had come from all over Italy to experience the festival. I must have passed it three times and was sobbing when I suddenly saw it and collected the pills. Corin was better when I got back, he took some pills and fell asleep. The next morning he had a large breakfast and said he felt fine. Going down the motorway my heart was in my mouth but we sailed along back to the little hamlet in the hills and nothing more was said until we got home to London. We went to see our GP, who picked up some irregularities with Corin's heart and suggested we went for a further examination at the hospital. We saw a top cardiologist at St George's, who found nothing to be concerned about. We didn't seek a second opinion.

That summer Corin opened as Lear at Stratford and after a short interval began working on *Tynan* with Richard Nelson. Either part, taken one at a time, would be extremely challenging for an actor, but to do both at once was physically and emotionally demanding. He was also very involved with the Guantanamo Human Rights Commission that he had formed the year before. At the same time we were busy founding the Peace and Progress Party, and campaigning for the release of Babar Ahmad, who was wrongly imprisoned in 2004 and was then in Woodhill Prison, under threat of extradition (he was extradited to the USA in 2012 without ever having been formally charged in Britain; another disgraceful act by a British Home Secretary).

After a regional tour, I was playing at the National Theatre in *The Permanent Way* by David Hare, directed by Max Stafford-Clark. This is a play based on the privatisation of the railways and the true accounts of people involved in the train crashes which followed from 1993-2002.

It included politicians, train company representatives, policemen, lawyers, and the victims themselves. It was a hugely compelling project and the first time that Hare and Stafford-Clark had collaborated for some years. It was also the first time that I had worked with either of them. Max asked me to audition for the part of Louise Christian, the human rights lawyer, which I did, and then I asked him if I could read the part of the author Nina Bawden, whose husband died in the Potters Bar crash. In the end Max gave me both parts, which was an honour because I liked and admired both women very much. When Corin died I had cause to re-read Nina's writing about grief which, although I had tried to interpret it as truthfully as I could at the time, was something I had not yet experienced.

Part II

CHAPTER TWELVE

JUNE 2005
Corin Collapses

O n 8 June 2005 our morning began with a press event at the Houses of Parliament to draw attention to the imminent eviction of the Dale Farm travellers from their site near Basildon in Essex.

During this time there had been an ongoing campaign to help the Roma people at Dale Farm. Whenever he could, Corin went down to visit them and we both took part in press campaigns. We had first got to know of their case through Rose Gentle, who had done some cleaning for me, and become a friend. I had given her daughter some reading lessons and had visited them on their site. She was very keen for me to see how clean their way of living was. They had been put onto a site which was next to open sewage, with little children running about. It was very unhealthy for them, but their caravans were spotless inside. Their great spokesman was Grattan Puxon who had been at Westminster School with Corin.

As we were leaving the hall after the press conference, one of the leading campaigners asked Corin to come down to Basildon to speak at the town hall; 'It will make all the difference to have you there in person,' she said. Corin had a great gift for speaking. He didn't use notes and he was articulate and passionate. He was always getting asked to speak at meetings. Sometimes there were two a week. That evening was a night off from *Pericles* which he had just opened at The Globe, so even though I supported this cause wholeheartedly I wasn't overjoyed when he told me he was going to Basildon Town Hall. We were due to have dinner with a new friend, Bill Bingham, at Rick's Café in Tooting. Corin was tired. *Pericles* had opened straight after *Tynan* and the rehearsals had been very demanding. But he never liked to say no so we went our separate ways, Corin to Basildon, and me to Tooting.

Coming back from the restaurant my mobile phone rang. It was a reporter from *The Independent*. 'Corin has been rushed to hospital after collapsing at a meeting in Basildon. Do you have a quote?' They didn't know if he was alive or not. Bill, who I'd been having dinner with, heroically drove me down to Basildon. We picked up Arden on the way. Corin was in intensive care, unconscious and on a life-support machine. One by one the other children arrived, and we camped in a little room outside the intensive care unit. While I didn't take it in, it seemed that Corin had suffered a heart attack, which left him without oxygen for more than three minutes. One of the travellers gave him mouth-to-mouth until the paramedics came, and most likely saved his life.

Later on the President of the Gypsy Council, Richard Sheridan, told me that before the meeting a local pub had refused to serve them, which had angered Corin. There was a heavy police presence at the town hall, and the atmosphere was highly charged. In the middle of an impassioned speech, Corin fell to the ground, unconscious.

There were several travellers from Dale Farm who were highly affected by what had happened, and who came to the hospital and waited in the corridors for news, as did our friends Sead and Bina Taslaman.

Kika's diary
Thursday 9 June 2005

Corin remains sedated all day and night. Harvey, Arden, me, Luke and Jemma stay all night in the little room. Pema, Lynn's eldest daughter, sings to him heart-rendingly.

In the morning his eyes open but don't see anything. Horrific.

He is not there.

Dr Lowe tells us that it's not a good outlook, the longer he doesn't recognise us, the worse the brain damage.

Some of the *Pericles* company: Kathryn Hunter, Marcello Magni and Patrice Naiambana arrive and join the family. Patrice sings his African song from *Pericles*; the one which he had sung to Corin to wake him from his sleep. Everyone claps, including nurses from other wards and some bemused patients.

Friday 10 June 2005

In the little room Dr Lowe tells me that there is no hope. There is a silence. I say, 'I hope you're wrong'. He says nothing and leaves. Jem puts her hand on my knee and I sit between the boys and we all sob hopelessly. The nurses say not to give up hope. I love them.

After two days of camping out in the little anteroom I come home to change my clothes. Barbara and Maggie, our kind neighbours, come round and bring wine. It wasn't till I unpacked the bag given to me by the nurses, and found his old brown wallet that I heard myself howling. Sally Simmons has taken time off work and is staying the night. I cannot believe I'll survive in this world without Corin.

This morning, when I go into the ward, Corin smiles at me like the sun in the sky. No inhibitions. From the soul. Naked. Not Corin, not anyone. No civilized grown-up could possibly smile like that. The smile takes over his face. A baby. I am horrified.

Roger Kirby, Corin's prostate specialist, and Peter Amoroso, Kirby's anaesthetist colleague, visit. They call themselves 'Batman and Robin' and encourage Dr Ekbal to remove the tube that makes Corin breathe. It's a life or death decision. As we stand around the bed and Corin manages to breathe naturally, without the life support, we all applaud.

Roger and Peter arranged for Corin to be moved to the Middlesex. Later we found out it took huge negotiations to do this because although Roger was his cancer surgeon he was not in charge of his heart treatment. I include here Roger's account of his experience of that time.

Professor Roger Kirby's Story

The call came through around 5.00 a.m., just as I disembarked at Athens airport to attend a meeting on prostate cancer.

'Roger, it's Kika. Corin has had a heart attack and is on a ventilator in Basildon Hospital. Can you help?'

'I'm in Greece,' I explained, 'but give me some more information and I'll see what I can do.'

Kika tearfully described Corin's cardiac arrest while addressing the gypsies in Basildon, followed by his prompt resuscitation by the St John's Ambulance team and then the transfer to hospital where a dire prognosis was given. What could I do? I was chairing a meeting of 1,000 invited delegates in the Intercontinental Hotel. I called Dr Peter Amoroso, my anaesthetic colleague. He rang the Intensive Care Unit at Basildon and spoke to the consultant-in-charge, who happened to be one of his former trainees, and who expressed a view that Corin had suffered severe brain damage from lack of oxygen to the brain after the cardiac arrest and that recovery was unlikely. The family, including Kika and Jemma, were by now at the bedside, but distraught with grief and disbelief.

I decided to ask a colleague to stand in for my last talk and leave the meeting early. I took an early morning flight back to Heathrow, stopped in briefly at my house in Wimbledon to pick up the car, and then drove hell for leather into the depths of Essex to Basildon, picking up Dr Peter Amoroso en route. Basildon hospital is a pretty unprepossessing place. A 1960s concrete monstrosity with a drab and untidy entrance manned by a surly porter who seemed disinclined to direct us to the Intensive Care Unit, but offered no objection to us proceeding in that general direction.

When we got there we found Kika and the family in despair.
There were also some of Corin's friends and fellow actors from
Pericles at the Globe where Corin was at the time playing
the main role. There was an all-pervasive atmosphere of deep
gloom, not lightened by the drab and gloomy ICU waiting
room that we found them in. 'Don't despair', I said, 'let's see
the patient and take it from there'.

It was essentially an anaesthetic and intensive care issue so
Peter took the lead. First he spoke to the consultant-in-charge
then he assessed Corin, who still had an endotracheal tube
in place and an intravenous infusion running, but who was
struggling and fighting the ventilator, which suggested that he
was ready to breathe for himself. It was time for the tube to
be removed from the trachea. So we assembled the family, and
with a flourish worthy of the Globe, Peter removed the tube
and allowed Corin to breathe spontaneously. He took several
enormous breaths and then sat up and smiled beautifully at
his assembled friends and family.

We left for London in the late afternoon and set about trying
to arrange a transfer to a hospital nearer Kika's home in
Wandsworth, and one with a good coronary care unit. The
Middlesex Hospital, at which I trained as a medical student
many years ago, agreed to take him and we managed to get an
ambulance to move him from Basildon into Central London.

He arrived drowsy, dazed and confused but still the unmistakable Corin. By this time he was speaking quite well and it was clear that his voice had not been affected by the episode but that his short-term memory was damaged. I told Kika that it would be a long haul and that he would never be quite the same again, but that progressive improvement could be anticipated.

CHAPTER THIRTEEN

JUNE 2005
Different Hospitals

R oger Kirby was as good as his word and got Corin transferred to the Middlesex Hospital where he remained in the intensive care unit until he could be moved to the Heart Hospital. It was much easier for the family to visit him there. This great hospital was facing imminent closure and was suffering from lack of facilities and staff but despite their grim surroundings we found the nurses' and doctors' care quite wonderful.

On the first evening visit I found him very confused but reassuringly Corin-like. He had already invited his new (and attractive) nurse Jenny, out to dinner with Harvey and his girlfriend, Jodie.

Kika's diary

Sunday 12 June 2005

He doesn't recognise me tonight and I can't settle him. He has not slept and is tired and fretful. Arms and legs turning into tortured positions which become rigid, then lifting them high above his head as if hanging from a tightrope. The symptoms are related to the impairment of the brain, one of the doctors tells me. Very, very disturbing. My sister Sonie visits when I am home and helps me answer calls, makes a soup. Oh my sister!

In the morning C says to me 'Lovely to see you... your nose is very nice.'

Me: 'Do you know who I am?'

C: 'Of course I know who you are.'

It's as if we are reading a script (possibly by someone masquerading as Beckett?) playing characters who don't seem to have a past or future or storyline. Only their tone of voice, the way they speak, gives a clue that they have shared each other's lives/a history at some time or other. A nurse asks what he would like to eat. 'Shotgun', he says.

Corin has soup, mince, pasta, potatoes and ice cream. I fed him by spoon and we managed well. At one point he asked if I'd had anything to eat. He tried to explain some of his memories of the five days. He knew people were helping him to survive. He wanted to 'press a button' and make it better. For the first time I had real hope that his intellect would remain intact. He said, 'It must have been difficult for you to manage.' 'It was,' I said. 'But we looked after one another.' 'It was difficult for me too,' he said.

Me at twelve years old with Coo Coo.

Michael Redgrave and David Markham in *The Stars Look Down*

My parents,
Olive and David. 1939.

Petra, Jehane, me and Sonia with our pets at Lear Cottage

Dad grooming one of the sows for the show.

Lear Cottage

Playing Viola in the modern-dress production of *Twelfth Night* at the Royal Court in 1968.

One of the images taken by Lord Snowdon, in a photoshoot for *The Sunday Times*.

Seen here as Carol the callgirl in *Double Dare* by Dennis Potter.

Feigning confidence at the start of filming with François Truffaut.

With Jean-Pierre Léaud in
scenes from *Les deux Anglaises et
le Continent* (Anne and Muriel).

Dad and Truffaut: laughing *with* me or at me?

The Committee of 100 sit down in Grosvenor Square against the Vietnam War. 1968.

I go to see him late at night. He is hot and uncomfortable and has slipped back. We have been visiting him too much and tiring him out. 'Slow, slow, slow' says Peter Amoroso.

Still awake at 4.00 a.m. Dreadful bleakness descends. I miss that cheery voice booming through the door, 'Hey darling!'

So tired but can't sleep. Listen to the Farming programme, which is becoming a comforting pastime. This morning is about the cruelty of intensive milk farming. Cows in their natural habitat produce twenty litres of milk, but now have drugs put into them to produce fifty litres, thus they are just 'milk machines', never getting to relax or go into the fields, their lifespan halved.

Corin tired and uncommunicative. He takes off his glasses to peer at my chin, something annoying he did, if a hair had appeared and I hadn't noticed... 'I should pull that out,' he says.

I pretend to hit him. He looks pleased.

I say I must go home and do some phoning. 'Why, have you had an offer?' he asks. Arden is sad because of a difficult time with Corin although Corin asked him what his plans were for the week which I thought was pretty good.

Corin was then moved to the Heart Hospital, to begin the next stage of his treatment. You have to take care of the heart first before they can address the problem of the brain damage. Dr McEwan, attractive, blonde, motherly and Scots, was his consultant. She explained they had found a blocked artery behind his heart, which they couldn't unblock but that they could put three other stents in and were discussing a defibrillator. They will have to do an angiogram, which is risky as it means being very still while staying conscious.

Kika's diary

Thursday 16 June 2005

This morning Corin is sitting up in a chair looking a bit deranged but oddly energetic. He has lost a lot of weight. He is staring intently at a box of Kleenex. Jemma and I read a card to him, from Lynn's daughter Pema. It is very complimentary. 'Crikey,' he says, then 'one gets wonderful lighting in hospitals….' Later, he asks if Rachel will be coming. A pause. My heart sank. Should I tell him the truth?

When I say 'No' he asks, 'Why not?'

A deafening pause. He doesn't remember. Oh God. Slowly I answer, 'Rachel died two years ago darling.'

Corin bursts into tears and cries piteously. This is terrible. I prayed that tears could be healing. That they could help bring some memory back. But no, apparently not.

This episode repeated itself with terrible freshness of sorrow each time, until an occupational therapist came to my rescue and taught me how to tell Corin about his mother. You have to start earlier on – remind him that she was ill for some time and pretty old, that he had been to see her shortly before she died, when she'd been staying with Natasha and Vanessa in America. When you see that he remembers that, you can gently arrive at the truth. 'Or,' as Peter A said, 'you can change the subject'. Something that hadn't occurred to me.

Corin says he is in a production where everything that can wrong, does. He tells the speech therapist he's been thrown into the scene without any preparation. A long, hot journey back to Balham. I have never felt so forlorn. Petra comes to the rescue and cooks a lovely supper and stays.

Kika's diary
Friday 17 June 2005

Corin looking thin and wild-eyed. The nurses have asked me to bring him some snacks and drinks as he isn't eating and is still losing weight. I give him the smoked salmon sandwiches I have made and he eats one straight off. I put them in the fridge. The nurse tells me that Corin remembered to ask for the sandwiches later.

Corin asks the nurse for a wine list! He still thinks he's in some kind of hotel in Singapore because of the beautiful Asiatic nurses. Believing that they're in a hotel seems to be a common response for people with brain injury. Reassuringly, he shows a fleeting interest in cricket. Bangladesh beating Australia....

Our chat is very fragmented and it's difficult to make conversation that isn't patronizing.

Monday 20 June 2005

Nightmare day. I go to see Corin to give him supper. Corin is wearing a gown, which only covers his front. The nurse is trying to get a dressing gown on him but he is trying to get to the loo and doesn't want to wait. He barely greets me. After twenty minutes I ask how much longer he's going to be.

'Corin!' 'WHAT IS IT?' 'How much longer?' 'I don't know.'

After a little more time he comes out and washes his hands which are red and sore-looking several times. There are wet scraps of paper towel everywhere. He complains that he doesn't have his make-up or towel or mascara. 'When do we start the Dress?' He's angry at the portable phone being taken away, which he thought belonged to him. His eyes are cold and he's worried, caught in the actor's nightmare of having to go on stage without knowing the part, no props, no preparation. I try to get him to eat supper but he snaps, 'I know what it is, thank you.' Dave, the Irish nurse, gets him to sit down and tells him unfortunately he's in a hospital. 'Oh,' says Corin. But he doesn't believe it. In the street I talk to Victor, the hospital caterer, who is Portuguese, and dresses like a waiter with dinner jacket and bow tie (no wonder Corin thinks it's a restaurant).

'People's memories go but they always remember what they love. That's why your husband thinks he's in a theatre! He will be alright tomorrow!'

The question I face is that perhaps Corin doesn't love me any more and won't ever be able to. He no longer looks at me as the Corin I know.

His eyes are neutral, cold and afraid.

Peter A says he has made an amazing 'physical' recovery but of the emotional and psychological healing, 'You haven't seen anything yet. You must have the patience of a saint and you mustn't get swamped. Slow, slow, slow....'

Tonight, Corin much more at ease. Sitting with the nurses at their desk and browsing through other patients' magazines. He recognised Tom O'Gorman, a long-standing friend, and Sally. Mostly he talked about meeting up with Paul Dehn, my uncle, the poet, screenwriter and critic, who would take Corin to previews as a boy.

Friday 24 June 2005

On the phone Corin tells me he thinks he's in a hospital.
I am overjoyed. Perhaps he's beginning to understand his
surroundings, but when I get to the ward after gridlocks,
thunderstorms etc., he is agitated and annoyed with the
speech therapist who he thinks is 'crude and amateurish…'

Rang Mark Rylance to thank him for his generosity in
keeping Corin on the payroll of the Globe after he had been
so horribly wrenched from the production of *Pericles*. He says
he thinks Corin's done all this so he can come back and use
the experience for his work!

Monday 27 June 2005

4.00 a.m. World Service. Listening to a debate on whether
whale hunting should be banned. Of course it should.

At this hour my mind tortures me with question after
question. Corin has three stents put in. He tells me I have
'two faces' but can't elaborate. Something that he admires
and to do with my acting. He thinks that Rachel is still alive
and he is convinced that being in hospital is 'a rebuke'. I am
worried about paying our tax and household bills. Will Corin
ever come back as himself or will I have to look after a grown-

up child for the rest of my life? He always wants champagne when visitors come. I hate it.

I try to concentrate on the:

Rose petal tea that Jemma bought me

'The Man Watching' – a poem by Rilke, sent by Mark Rylance

My wombat from Sydney

Mutchka the cat

Harvey and Arden, Jemma and Luke

Sonie, Petra and Jehane, my dearest sisters

They will, and do… comfort me…

Tuesday 28 June 2005

Vanessa flew in this morning and had a joyful meeting with Corin. All the while she and Lynn have been in different shows in New York and we have kept in touch by telephone. In the little room that Corin inhabits she unrolled an enormous length of green and gold cloth that had been worn by Martha Graham – possibly as Hecuba? – the role that Vanessa's just played – and draped it round and round and round me.

Corin has had a defibrillator put in – a difficult procedure – leaving a sore-looking weal on his right shoulder. He became very agitated that night not knowing where Rachel was. Jemma rang and we decided that one of us needed to go into the hospital the next morning. Harvey says he will go, and I get to bed finally, stress level 100 and climbing.

Wednesday 29 June 2005

Corin very subdued and depressed.

I am awake at 3.00 a.m.

There is nothing to look forward to anymore. I am worried about mortgage payments and C's tax in January.

I am worried about him coming home although he must come home. But I've no idea how I'll manage.

Very lonely.

Thursday 30 June 2005

Corin and I talk about being in *King Lear* and *Pericles* and their 'journeys' of discovery. Losing themselves, or being lost to the world. How Corin's journey was a real one and how interesting it would be, he could write about it and tell us what it had been like. At the moment he doesn't remember anything about either production.

Jason, the Irish Staff nurse, says Corin is very clever and bluffs a lot of the time.

Corin had written about *King Lear* earlier that year, before his cardiac arrest:

'My first encounter with *King Lear* was at Stratford more than half a lifetime ago. I was thirteen.

'...My second encounter was when I played Lear for Radio 3 in 2001. Remembering that my mother had played Regan to my father's Lear, the director Cherry Cookson asked my wife, Kika Markham, to play her for the broadcast.

'I had been diagnosed recently with prostate cancer and had begun a course of drug therapy in preparation for six weeks of radiotherapy. Prostate cancer develops from an imbalance of testosterone, and in essence the chemical treatment, which in my case was a drug called Casodex, works by inhibiting the production of testosterone. Over time this enhances a man's secondary female characteristics. My hair, which had been slowly and steadily thinning since I left university, started to thicken. My chest hair became fine and downy instead of coarse and thick.

'These feminising traits, with others that are even less welcome, are reversed when the treatment is over. But they were only beginning when we started to record *Lear*. I was aghast. Nothing in the literature, nor in the accounts of fellow patients, had prepared me for the psychological effect of these changes. I hated my drug. It was a large round white tablet, and so powerful that it seemed to kick me in the chest, five minutes after swallowing it. I had heard of patients who were still taking the drug years after the onset of the illness, and I swore to myself that I would stop taking it after the radiotherapy, whatever the consequences. (I did stop, and am still going strong.)

'So at one level, and thanks to Cherry Cookson's production, I have a deeper and more personal understanding of Lear than I might have acquired at some other time. It is this: Lear has a great fear of the feminine side of his nature. At every critical juncture in the conflict with his daughters, his anxiety and dread are that he will betray his masculinity by crying, and when that happens he is devastated.

Lear: I'll tell thee:
> (*To* GONERIL.)
> Life and death! I am ashamed
> That thou hast power to shake my manhood thus;
> That these hot tears, which break from me perforce,
> Should make thee worth them. Blasts and fogs upon thee!
> Th'untented woundings of a father's curse
> Pierce every sense about thee!

'Lear is terrified of the mother, i.e. the woman, within him:

> Oh, how this mother swells up toward my heart!
> Hysterica passio, down thou climbing sorrow!

'Scholarly notes explain that according to ideas of anatomy at this time, hysterica passio begins in the womb (hysteria in Greek), and climbs, via the heart, to the patient's throat, suffocating him. Yes, but Lear's invocation also describes perfectly how I was hit in the chest by Casodex, and the psychological trauma of being overcome by the woman inside.

'Perhaps it was because of these experiences with Casodex, or maybe because of a son's inevitable wish to do things differently from his father and establish his superiority, that I found I could remember almost nothing of his performance when I came to play Lear last year at the RSC. Only the wig and the costume, the cursing of his daughters and the final entry with Cordelia in his arms.

'With Annie [Castledine], with whom I had often worked, I began a correspondence that continued on and off throughout rehearsal.

'She made me think about Lear... Absolute power has robbed him of the facility of imagination, the ability to see himself as others see him, or empathise with others. It has divorced him from his inner life, so that he has no soliloquy, no irony, no self-awareness. And only in and through catastrophe and madness, at great cost to others and himself, does he become human.'

The Guardian, Monday 17 January 2005

Kika's diary
Friday 1 July 2005

A lovely message from Phil Quast, the actor and singer we both love and admire, and who, with Corin, ran weekly poetry readings against the Iraq war in the upstairs foyer of the National Theatre. I wish I could have called him back, but he's in the Australian outback somewhere.

Today I told Corin what happened on 8 June. The press conference leading to the meeting at Basildon. Where he'd had the heart attack having become very emotional while giving the speech. He wrote it all down, said it was very helpful, read it back three times very accurately. At the moment he is not retaining the idea that he's in hospital. He dutifully repeats it and has 'learnt' that he's in the Heart Hospital. He wanted me to get 'the script' which was

Macbeth. I couldn't get the play on its own, so got the whole
works, a large unwieldy volume, but he didn't mind, and
seemed to enjoy reading *Macbeth.* Earlier he was agitated. We
went down to Raffles coffee shop with Arden and Petra. He
was in the old pattern of anxiously worrying about rehearsing
and schedules and plans etc. I realised I'd been there seven
hours. I think it's too long. Very, very, very depressed. Talked
to Terry Waite. Cried to Marina Voikhanskaya, a Russian
doctor who my father helped and who has stayed a friend of
the whole family ever since. Russians understand suffering
and never patronise. The one bright spot is Arden passing all
the units in his second year at university. What a triumph!

At the end of June the biggest dilemma was the next stage of Corin's
treatment and what it should be. Was he too unstable to come home
without nursing supervision? And had he possibly forgotten that he
ever had a home? This was a horrible thought. We needed to get him
to a place that could help restore the memory and begin to heal the
psychological trauma he'd had. We didn't understand at that point
that the brain was far too inflamed and swollen to be able to respond
to a programme of rehabilitation. He needed 'containment and re-
orientation' – something that had begun on a small scale with the
occupational therapists at the Heart Hospital – and above all, time for
the brain to heal itself.

We had heard that the best chance of appropriate treatment would
be at the National Hospital for Neurology and Neurosurgery in Queen
Square, Bloomsbury. An important factor was that a patient who has
suffered brain injury, memory loss etc., will never want to go back into
hospital once they have been home. Therefore, to bring him home too
quickly could be very risky. I was cracking under the strain of guilt, and

missing discussing all this with Corin. After researching and asking a lot of professionals what choices were open to us, we put all our hopes into the hospital at Queen Square. We were given an appointment with Dr Hickman on 4 July.

Tuesday 5 July 2005

Wake up, still feel terrible. Cry to anyone who is kind. Margot, Jim MacKeith, think I'm having a breakdown.

There is caviar, lemon, yoghurt, honey on Corin's table from Vanessa. Lots of visitors. Roger Michell reads *Macbeth* with Corin.

Vanessa comes back with poached sea bass and broccoli that she's cooked for Corin.

Later I take a Librium and stay awake all night.

Wednesday 6 July 2005

Upstairs in Corin's room there are white peaches, an ice box, smoked salmon, yoghurt, mangoes, honey and a small pot of caviar. I feel a lot of support coming from Vanessa. In more ways than one. We all go to The Garden Café in Regent's Park and sit in deckchairs while she tells Corin and I about *Hecuba*. Very peaceful. Later in the discussion with a family psychiatrist she defends me. We are struggling over the question of whether Corin comes home for a visit or not. Luke says it's not about me but about Dad. Vanessa says it is absolutely about me. She holds my hand.

CHAPTER FOURTEEN

SUMMER 2005
Corin Comes Home

There were three choices open to us, two on the NHS, and one private. The Oliver Zangwill Centre for Neuropsychological Rehabilitation, run by Barbara Wilson, is a clinic in Ely, Cambridgeshire that is privately open to patients from outside the borough.

We went down to visit the team and liked the staff and head doctor, but in order to take part in the rehab programme, you had to live out in a B&B, come in every morning and look after yourself in the evenings, i.e. something that would demand a lot more independence than Corin had then. The Wolfson was nearest to us and also highly recommended, and then there was the National at Queen Square, Bloomsbury.

We tried the National first, but after an interview with Dr Hickman the medical team decided he was not suitable (for treatment with them) so we then sought an interview at the Wolfson. They wanted him to stay as an in-(house)patient with supervised home visits, which seemed dreadfully cruel. Later we understood the reason for this and paid the price for Corin being an outpatient, as the shorter hours meant he wasn't able to have the eight-hour intensive rehabilitation needed to re-orientate him. We were still novices when it came to treatment of brain injury. All this time, Corin was still at the Heart Hospital, and it was becoming obvious that he needed more emotional and psychological help. We went back to Queen Square and waited until they were able to accept him as an in-patient. It was the only option open to us and we were relieved and grateful.

Corin had just moved into the hospital on 6 July when the catastrophic London bombs went off the very next day – one close by near Tavistock Square, which Corin must have heard. There was no transport anywhere so I walked to the hospital – the streets were full of walking silent people – no buses or taxis, just worried-looking people. I longed to be able to talk to Corin about what had happened but thought it would upset him, so I said nothing. When 9/11 happened I was in Northampton playing *A Wedding Story* by Bryony Lavery. I don't know where C was but we rang each other every two hours – we thought it was the beginning of World War Three.

At first Corin seemed to settle down on the small comfortable ward with green curtains surrounding each bed and a small locker. But every morning he would wake, unsure which country he was in. Sometimes, he thought he was in Vienna, which was strange until I realised he'd been reading the Thomas Bernhard script *Heldenplatz* which we had had translated by Andrea Tierney and were both going to be in.

Tuesday 12 July 2005

I brought Corin a review of *Pericles* in The *Independent*. He read it.

'It's recent?'

'Yes, do you remember it?'

'Sort of.'

In the Raffles shop he says, 'So it's not on now?'

'Yes it is. It's still going on.'

'Who's going on for me?'

'Mark Rylance, with the book.'

'Well that's an honour I suppose.'

I came to the hospital every day and we sat at the long refectory table for lunch with the tall arched windows looking out onto Queen Square. Corin was becoming sadder all the time. One of the activities we did together was to look at his 'Get Well' cards and start to answer them. He read them very carefully and was very touched by some, in particular Babar Ahmad's card from Woodhill Prison. But soon he became restless and listless and very confused as to where he was – Italy?

The hospital says he could come home for a short visit with the family to see how it goes.

Dreadful scary night. Fall asleep without sleeping pill at midnight and wake at 2.00 a.m. I am at the bottom of a lake. Unnamable sadness. Is it loneliness? Take pill. So apprehensive about Corin coming home.

Saturday 16 July 2005

It's Corin's 66th birthday and he arrives home and is very pleased – relieved? – to see me. Hugs me for a long time. Seems happy to be in the kitchen and garden but he takes no notice of his surroundings. Looks at all of his cards very carefully. We go out in the garden.

I show him the apples growing well, but he shows little interest in them or the garden. Doesn't go upstairs. Doesn't stroke Mutchka our beloved cat and at 3.30 becomes restless and wants to go back to hospital. How terrible and sad. And a relief. The children suffer for him and want him to come home properly. I am torn between wanting to please them and feeling horribly afraid of having to look after him in this situation. He reveals so little of his dilemma. I suppose he cannot articulate it. After all, he still doesn't believe he's had a heart attack.

Mark Rylance sends Corin a lovely card:

> *Corin*
>
> *Happy Birthday my old friend. Every day, every moment, every blink of the eye — A Birthday in your wide and universal life.*
>
> *It was grand to see you and I got so much from our conversation about what it is that connects people. We talked of these days now being like the first rehearsal weeks of a new part, a new role for you. I'm so happy to be in this play with you. I sense you have been somewhere words can't describe, but being with your patience and thoughtful nature gave me a feeling of it.*
>
> *Lots of love and Happy Birthday.*
>
> *Mark*

Thursday 21 July 2005

Another bomb scare. All the stations are closed. Everyone walking. Went to Chiswick with Vanessa who gave me a lovely chicken salad with chutney, and jelly and cream! Corin rings sounding sad and frail. Says his session with the psychologist was hateful. I begin crying – again. Vanessa very kind and drives me back into London. Most of the roads are blocked off so I get out and walk to the hospital. When I get there I see Corin helping patients and visitors into taxis, gaily, acting as a doorman, 'Have a good evening! Good night!' It's kind of sweet and scary at the same time. Brain injury causes disinhibition, which I intend to learn a lot more about. He wants to come home, and there is pressure from the family for him to stay the night, which makes me resentful. I'm frightened because I don't know who he is any longer and what he might do. I don't have enough medical knowledge to cope with another possible episode. As it happens, his psychologist says it will not be good for Corin to come home to stay at this point. It will only confuse him and he will not want to go back to hospital, and it will be impossible to continue his treatment. So the home visit is delayed.

Saturday 23 July 2005

Get to the hospital around 5 p.m. to find Corin fast asleep.

At supper the nurse wakes him and he becomes or is extremely depressed. 'I'm falling apart'. We eat supper on the ward, cauliflower cheese, and do some replies to his cards. He does this very well, but loses interest. Wants to go home. Becomes distant and morose. Looks as if he wants to cry but can't. I tell him these feelings are a sign of recovery. He has pain when rehearsing a part and but now it's his life. It helps a bit but now we are both distressed. A walk round the square helps. The nurses are kind to me and hug me which makes me cry. Later blessed Vanessa rings.

Afternoon, Tuesday 26 July 2005

Watching the film in the ward. Corin and I both weeping, watching Emma Thompson and Alan Rickman in a Jane Austen movie. Luckily Harvey comes by and cheers us both up by showing us his diamond engagement ring for Jodie. 'Ann', one of the patients, is an expert on jewellery, particularly diamonds, studies it carefully and pronounces the carat. Delightful moment.

Wednesday 27 July 2005

The pain I feel now is the happiness I had before. That's the deal.

C.S. Lewis

Terrible loneliness coming home on the tube. No one in the kitchen. No one in the garden. Jemma rings up and cancels coming over. About to drown in weeping. Have a whisky. Put a chicken in the casserole.

Friday 29 July 2005

When I come into the ward, Ann tells me that Corin was very agitated in the morning and told her to go to rehearsal to check her lines.

Apparently, they were doing *Three Sisters* – Corin said he didn't need to look at his lines as he'd been understudying the play all his life!

Happiness comes when the family arrive and take Corin through the little park to local Italian trattoria Cosmoba. The waiters are very friendly and particularly love it when Vanessa, who speaks perfect Italian, orders the food and chats to them.

Sunday 31 July 2005

Lunch with Harvey and Jodie. It went well. Corin had a lovely sleep on their double bed. Then on to Vanessa in King Edward VII Hospital waiting for an operation. Vanessa looking wonderful in black retro dress of Joely's, glasses and straight hair.

On leaving, Corin becomes VERY agitated and thought we were due to be at a production meeting with the director and others. He said later 'I feel an awful fool.'

Monday 1 August 2005

Corin rings me from hospital at 8.00 a.m. and cries. My heart is breaking. How long can we go on like this?

Harvey rings to say he has proposed to Jodie – on the beach – and she has accepted!

Corin rings to say he has packed for home and when am I coming to get him? I cannot convince him he's in a hospital and must stay for treatment. 'Well when are you coming?'

He has become, in the course of the morning, very angry and paranoid. His psychologist has tried to calm him but to no avail, and by the time I get there he refuses to sit anywhere and talk, even outside, because it is 'dangerous' and there is a state conspiracy to murder us, 'we must get away.'

We walk round and round the little park, he refusing to go back to the hospital and gripping me tightly. Then he hails a taxi and pulls me in beside him. 'We're going home.'

The nurses are by this time gathered round and trying to get me out of the taxi. Corin is threatening violence to anyone who tries to stop us. I manage to tell the taxi driver to keep driving round the area for a bit. The driver realises what has happened and after a bit we end up at the hospital entrance again. By this time, two consultants are there and they ask Corin to come in and talk. They are calm and sympathetic but Corin is angry and won't be pacified. They want to take him to the psychiatric wing upstairs, but Corin won't get in the lift. I'm sure that one of us is going to have a heart attack or faint. Corin is very red in the face and convinced that they are State police. Eventually he comes with the doctors up to the fifth floor and we all have a cup of tea.

They explain to us that they will have to keep him in a closed ward for some weeks and monitor him, but this may be against his will.

Vanessa bravely says that she is prepared to take him home with her and to look after him.

They warn us that once out of hospital, Corin will never agree to come back again.

I couldn't think what to do for the best. But I couldn't bear the thought of leaving him in a closed ward.

So that night, we take Corin back to Vanessa's flat in Chiswick.

We give him some valium and put him to bed.

I, too, take a valium, but I don't sleep. We have cut loose from all medical supervision or help. I am frightened.

Later, Dr B explains to Corin and me just how distressing memory loss is and how it can lead to mental breakdown. When in everyday life one feels lost or disturbed, or in a place we don't recognise, we use reflective, self-monitoring memory to re-orientate ourselves back to reality.

But if we are unable to reflect or remember past events it is traumatic. We may not feel 'normal' but we don't think we have gone mad – we don't quite know (a few weeks ago Corin and I talked a lot about *King Lear* and Corin's present situation) so we think that all the problems and danger are coming from the outside, the other people. You become paranoid and/or psychotic.

Corin was coping with cognitive difficulties, not physical ones. As an actor he was very good at hiding these difficulties. Helping him adjust to what had been lost is part of the struggle that we all engaged in.

AUGUST 2005
Springfield

T wo days after Corin moved in with Vanessa, I was door-stepped by the *Daily Mail* who wanted to know if my marriage was over as Corin was now living with her. Despite all my experience of the tabloid press, I'm afraid I was still shocked and distressed at the cynicism of it. 'Is this why you wanted to become journalists?' I shouted at them, 'To increase people's unhappiness? Even if you're not ashamed, your mother would be…' Oh dear. I should have lived in another century.

After a day of not being able to leave the house without them appearing from behind the privet hedge (there must have been very little happening in the news that week), I rang Harvey's best friends Joe Edmonds and Tom Brind who lived nearby and asked if they could come over. This they did and guarded the house until the wretched scavengers retreated with no story to tell. Tom and Joe were the 'men of the match' that day and I will never forget their kindness to me.

The next three weeks were rather surreal. We all took turns staying at Vanessa's so that one of us was always around in case of difficulties that might arise with Corin. He and I would walk along Chiswick Mall past the lovely Bedford House overlooking the river, where his family had lived for a time, and then to the Black Lion pub for lunch and watch the cricket.

Corin's Diary
Sunday 14 August 2005

My second visit of the day. We arrive about 1.00 p.m., as
England plough, not very successfully, through their second
attack. No hook on the lavatory door to hang one's jacket on.
But too much bustle and noise at the bar to complain.

Kika has a lager and lime. Very nice. I joined her. Delicious.
After lunch we lay down half hopeful of sleep, but for
some reason it didn't come. So many thoughts jostled for
expression on the way back, but too many to be remembered.
It was lovely to walk with Kika on a Sunday. Something to
remember and bear in mind for the future. With her I can be
happy. That's my best thought for the day!!!!!

But sometimes he would confuse me with Deirdre his first wife and
would ask where Kika was… One day Vanessa invited Petra over for a
fantastic lunch. Tomato and mozzarella salad, floury potatoes, poached
salmon with an Elizabeth David amazing green sauce and stewed
mulberries from Eileen Atkins's garden with cream! She told us about a
disastrous trip to China she had once made and we were mesmerised.

Another day we listened to a radio play by Corin, *My Sister Under
the Skin*, based on a real event about a woman who believed she was
Corin's half-sister. Corin is moved to tears by the story, and me as
Sylvia, and had completely forgotten that he wrote it.

I don't know if Corin understood why he was staying at Vanessa's.
He doesn't like it when I go back to Balham and indeed it's gut-
wrenchingly horrible when I have to say goodbye.

Vanessa says that his not going home is depressing him, and I'm aware that all the family want him to come back to Balham, so I feel under enormous pressure.

Kika's diary

Monday 15 August 2005

Fear of being stuck. Trapped forever! Trying to find a way to move forward.

On the positive side I like helping him, but I don't like 'nursing'. Guilt at being cross and wanting to escape. Guilt at my shortcomings. The irritation of Corin mixing me up with Deirdre and forgetting he's seen me.

Not making his own cup of tea. Walking in small steps – is he exaggerating his frailty? When I point it out to him he suddenly zooms ahead with great long strides and I have to run after him. The old Corin…

Sometimes I wonder if he's faking the whole thing.

Not being able to grieve for him *as he was*.

Too painful. Again denial. This is not happening.

We succeeded in getting an interview again with the
Wolfson, but they were wary of taking Corin in because of
the incident at Queen Square. Anyway, Corin didn't want
to come as a live-in patient, and, 'Unless the patient feels
the need to have treatment and has the will to want to work
with the OTs (occupational therapists) it will not succeed –
better to wait until he is ready,' said Martin van den Broek,
the chief consultant at the Wolfson.

Corin talks ceaselessly throughout the interview, an angry
stream of words – 'People pay to see me... I am special, I am
a genius... and 'specialist'. Not like others. I am a soloist, a
musician. But nobody understands the music I'm playing!'
He is very angry.

Van den Broek listens attentively, and sympathetically never
patronises. He impresses me, he's detached and professional.

After the interview, Corin bursts into tears. I try to comfort
him by saying that we're on a journey of discovery together;
it's not just him alone, that he will find new parts of himself,
that it's a 'process'. This word seems to comfort him. Harvey
arrives and gives calm practical and sympathetic advice.
He, too, is coping with worry and sadness about his dad's
condition. I am so proud of him.

We all thought work was a key factor in Corin's recovery.
After a few months Vanessa took Corin to meet with John
Barton who was writing *The War That Still Goes On*, based
in part on Thucydides' *The History of the Peloponnesian War*.
Corin starts to work with John and enjoys it hugely. It's his
first work since the heart attack and the first time I see him
happy. The paradox in the background is that he has no idea
where we live or what our address is, or even where Balham
is. His world is entirely with Barton and Vanessa. However
it became clear that it was too early on in his illness to begin
work. Corin found it too hard to sustain his concentration.
He never got to perform the readings.

We drive down to Lear Cottage on Ashdown Forest to see
my mother with Vanessa. Mum adores her and Corin. She is
quite frail today, and has hurt her arm from one of her strange
shaky attacks. Vanessa makes her a sling very deftly out of the
scarf she wore as Hecuba, and my mother wears it with great
pride, in fact for days after. Corin, looking pale and tired,
sleeps in the old fat green armchair in the dark sitting room
by the fireplace. I sit on the grass under the pine tree's shade
and Mum sits on a chair. We have a cry and hug each other.

'God, Mum, we're both crying.' 'I know,' she says, 'isn't
it lovely.'

Monday 22 August 2005

Very sad, very near the edge, can't stop crying. Big Jehane [West] said I'm grieving for the old Corin and haven't got used to, or don't yet know, the new one.

I felt too ill to go to Chiswick and stay at home to encourage Arden and Vedran Taslaman (his best friend), who are painting the spare room and putting up shelves to make it into a study for Corin, something he's always wanted. From the kitchen I can hear a lot of arguing and laughter from them, which is very cheerful. The talent for DIY is severely lacking in both the Redgrave and Markham families, whereas Vedran, an engineer of promise, can do it in his stride. This afternoon, the garden is filled with theatrical bric-a-brac; boxes of books, photographs, pictures, which we have to either find a place for or throw out. I must be mad to try and do all this before Corin comes back.

Thursday 25 August 2005

Lovely evening with Corin. He talks about writing a play or account of a man who's lost his mind but is trying to re-find reality. We sleep in the same bed, an awful bucket but very friendly and comforting being together.

3.00 a.m. I am waiting for the sleeping pill to work
and listening to Retha Hofmeyr talking about how she
uses tortoises to research climate change. We have had a
catastrophe and Corin is in Charing Cross Hospital. Earlier
this evening, at Chiswick, Corin took me into his bedroom
and asked me what drugs he was being given. He pointed to
the wardrobe saying he could hear voices. I opened the door
and showed him that there were just clothes hanging there.
His eyes looked frightened, rolling a little – icy. I managed
to get Vanessa and their cousin Robin Kempson, who was
staying with her, on their own and tell them that I was
frightened about the way Corin was acting, and was going
home with Tom who would drive me back.

This was the sequence of events:

Kika's diary
Friday 26 August 2005

Sometime after I left, Corin, now believing Vanessa and
Robin to be his 'enemies', walks out of the house and into
the road, threatening them with violence if they try to stop
him. An ambulance is called by Vanessa, but he won't go in
it unless he is accompanied by police, and he wants their

protection. He then manages to flag down a bus (it's now about 10.00 p.m.) and gets on it, followed by Robin who starts to explain to the driver to wait until the ambulance comes as Corin is unwell.

The driver thinks it is Robin who has gone off the rails as he is wearing a green towelling dressing gown and slippers (he'd gone to bed early).

The driver tells the passengers to get off the bus and the policeman manages to reassure Corin and go with him to Charing Cross Hospital. Later, Vanessa rings me and tells me to come to the hospital straight away. She doesn't say why and I think Corin has had another heart attack and sob all the way there in the taxi. Corin is in an anteroom somewhere.

I could hear him asking to be released. My heart was cracking; Vanessa's too. He must have felt so alone and scared. We were told not to see him as it would distress him more, and advised by a senior medical consultant that Corin needed to be under constant supervision which would probably mean having to section him, as he did not think Corin would stay anywhere voluntarily. He suggested Springfield University (Mental) Hospital as it was near our house and it would be easier to visit him. They also said it would be less confusing if Corin were taken there without Vanessa or me and promised that the nurses would be very kind to him.

Robin came back home with me and slept in the spare room. Vanessa went home alone, and Corin was taken to Springfield Hospital.

* * *

September 2005

Corin's time in Springfield was so traumatic for us all that I couldn't even write about it at the time. He had a tiny room with a bed and a chest of drawers. There were bars on the window, not unlike a prison cell, or a room in a workhouse. I brought him bedspreads, cushions, photos, and mugs from home to brighten it. His moods were extreme and unpredictable: from black despair through elation to anger. He was greatly helped by the kindness of Professor Ian Robbins who came and talked to him, listened to him and comforted him. I have still to thank him for this.

Although Corin doesn't consciously remember any of his time at Springfield, two years later when he performed Wilde's *De Profundis*, I understood that the sorrow and truth in his portrayal was not 'acted' but had been experienced at a deep level.

I only have to think of Corin, face at the window, behind bars, and my chest tightens; I stop being able to breathe, even now. It is truly terrible to see a distinguished-looking 'civilised' older man crying without restraint in bitterness and sorrow because he cannot understand what is going on or why he is being held prisoner. It must have confirmed all his worst fears.

I came to deeply respect the nurses at Springfield. Again, these dedicated people who deal with mental traumas and appalling psychological difficulties in shabby, primitive Victorian buildings, are true heroes.

I liked the way his consultant, Dr Hughes, Irish and softly spoken, talked to Corin in a compassionate and direct manner. Corin liked the food well enough: meat pie and two veg, and jam roll and custard. Having been at a public school had made him very unfussy about food – unlike me.

He made friends and started smoking roll-ups with them in the small grassy area outside, where you could sit on a bench and feed the sparrows. I remember one late September day my brother-in-law, Roger Lloyd-Pack, Jehane, Corin and I took a rug and had a picnic there, and talked about theatre.

After some weeks, he was encouraged to come home for afternoon visits, and on one of those days I was alarmed to hear him shouting for me to come quickly. He was standing over the loo which was filled with blood. Both of us nearly fainted. I called an ambulance and he was rushed to St George's Hospital, which we knew only too well. He had been treated there for prostate cancer by Roger Kirby, and this time some of the nurses remembered him. He'd had a crush on a beautiful nurse from Lagos, Nigeria and had written *Saint Lucy*, a searing, truthful and funny play about it and what it was like to have prostate cancer. Aicha Kossoko played the nurse and I played his wife. I was never so happy as when he was writing a play because it meant that he stayed at home, and that I got to have a juicy part as well!

Luckily, the horrifying amount of blood was not as dangerous as it appeared. He was soon ready to leave hospital and I made arrangements for him to come home. The need to look after him became stronger than the earlier fear of what could happen – brain injury is unseen and unknowable. Blood, vomit or shit are your friends in comparison.

CHAPTER SIXTEEN

OCTOBER 2005
Rehab

Once home, Corin was inclined to stay in bed all day until, after much prompting, he would sometimes come downstairs to dinner. But wherever he was, in bed, on the sofa downstairs, or sitting under the tree in the garden, he kept very, very still. Not a muscle moved. His eyes wide open, thinking, puzzling, puzzling and thinking. What had plunged him into this darkness, this half-world? He who 'knew everything' now understood nothing. It must have been a terrible suffering, yet he never complained.

The one thing he couldn't bear was noise. People talking, the television and radio. I couldn't even play music, something we had both listened to every day of our lives. The world became silent. I cooked and washed up as he sat in silence at the kitchen table.

I swung from anguish to rage to wanting to laugh. We seemed like figures in a bad production of Strindberg. For the first time in our relationship we were unable to communicate with one another through familiar ways. We waited like orphans until our guardian angels, Harvey and Jodie, came back from work. They were staying with us until 'things settled down', and the moment they came through the door the atmosphere became easier.

I dreaded the moment when it was time for Corin's pills as he didn't understand why he should take them. He still didn't believe that he'd had a heart attack. Sometimes he thought I was part of a conspiracy and was trying to kill him and would throw them across the room. Often, it wasn't until I'd rung our GP at his home and got him to talk to Corin and explain that he'd had a heart attack that he would accept his medication.

Eventually, in desperation, I rang Springfield. They explained this was a common occurrence following brain injury and that they would send the 'Team' around. The 'Team' consisted of two nurses, I think Malaysian, man and woman, who had a sort of relaxed authority and could sum up the situation in a flash. You wouldn't want to mess with them. They arrived at 8.30 p.m. 'Hello Mr Redgrave! We have your pills for you now'. And Corin would take them, meek as a lamb and bid them good night with a friendly wave, seeing them to the door. This happened every night for several weeks.

I put my head round the bedroom door. 'Do you feel like getting up?'

There are a hundred ways of asking this, a hundred tones of voice. This time I had an encouraging tone.

'Soon...' And as I sigh, and trudge back downstairs, his beautiful unchanged voice floats down, 'And I genuinely mean SOON!'

At first I was Corin's full-time carer. Then through Equity, my union, we received a life-saving amount of money every month, from the Royal Theatrical Fund and the Actors' Benevolent Fund, to pay for a carer. Brendan was a capable, sensitive man who was trained as an actor and a nurse, specialising in mental health care: a useful combination.

On one occasion Corin, not remembering who Brendan was, threatened to punch him if he did not get out of his bedroom. Brendan wasn't fazed. He did a fair stint with us. Then he was offered an acting job. It was now down to me to be a full-time carer again.

We weren't getting any rehab yet. Corin didn't have a reason to get up. Having a shower was complete misery as he hadn't regained his co-ordination and balance and felt clumsy. The most telling thing was that he no longer cared about his appearance. He was very depressed – and cross; we both were. When he did eventually come into the kitchen for his dinner, still in his dressing gown, he admonished me in a clear voice:

'This is going to end in divorce Kika.'

'OK then,' I would answer, in a horrid, bright voice.

I was warned by Peter Amoroso and a consultant at the Heart Hospital that one should try *not* to be the chief carer, as it would be detrimental to our relationship. I shouldn't try to be his memory or let him become dependent on me. *His* independence was paramount.

I wasn't adjusting – I was so, so full of grief, self-pity and rage that Corin couldn't comfort me. He needed comfort so much himself. During all this time Corin's consultants at Springfield and the Wolfson were constantly adjusting his medication, which was crucial in helping him live as normally as possible. There were signs that he was in the depths of despair. A photo of him holding my mother's hand at the cottage in Sussex is unbearably sad. At Christmas 2012 I found two scraps of paper, undated, from one of his journals, which fluttered out from one of his favourite books, *Austerlitz* by W.G. Sebald:

> Even Glenn Gould, our friend and the most important piano virtuoso of the century, only made it to the age of fifty-one, I thought to myself as I entered the Inn.
>
> *The Loser*, Thomas Bernhard

> *Suicide calculated well in advance, I thought, no spontaneous act of desperation.*
>
> *The Loser*, Thomas Bernhard

His writing is shaky and small, which is how it was in the first year of illness. How I wish I had found them before. Suicide? Perhaps we could have talked about it, but then again... perhaps not.

On one occasion Vanessa and I had both been trying to get him up, with no success. We were in the kitchen and I was preparing a tray of breakfast to take upstairs. I didn't want him to take pills on an empty stomach.

'Do you think that a good idea?' she asked.

I reacted wildly: 'Don't criticise me so quickly, we'll never manage to live together...' (an idea we had discussed some while back).

'But he's not like that with me. It's because you look so anxious all the time and you haven't got a ROUTINE!'

It was all true, which didn't help. It was another thing that I was being endlessly advised on, 'Get a Routine, a *structure!*' God, how I hated those words. I had avoided routines all my life, except in the WRP and, of course, when rehearsing a play. I was forced to admit I needed a daily plan of some sort now. But a group of friends were already becoming part of our daily pattern. There was hardly a day when Tom didn't turn up, either to run us to the hospital, or clean the kitchen or watch Arsenal on TV. Our Bosnian friends Bina and Sead came often. We had always walked together in the evenings, and Corin and Sead had played tennis to the bitter end, both men being highly competitive. We had three Commons to choose from: Tooting, where we had taken the boys when they were little, and was closest to home; Battersea; and Wandsworth. On our first walk in Battersea Park, Corin asked where we were. He didn't recognise anything. Not even the river. Or Battersea Power Station. We could have been in Vienna or Budapest – we were walking in European parks not English ones, like a Hitchcock film where you have no idea where you are but it's so familiar to everyone else that you think you are mad. And sometimes Corin did think that.

A new and worrying development. Corin started to have falls: it was very alarming, as he had begun to venture out to the shops or pub on his own. Mostly the falls happened when I was around. Once down a flight of ninety steps in Harley Street. I thought he was dead, lying with a gash on his forehead, completely still, but within minutes he'd got up. As it was Harley Street there was not a single person who could help us, none of them were insured. So Jemma, who was nearby, went into The London Clinic and up to a ward and got some dressings which Sonie and I put on back in Balham.

There were many other falls. One on a trip to see my mother, whom we were visiting often as she was becoming more frail. Some outside the house and some inside. One very bad one in the kitchen which caused a violent nose bleed. We were rushed to A&E. It took two hours for Corin to be seen – me holding his nose all the while – his mouth full of dried blood.

The doctors were tired and overworked, finally cauterising the nostrils and discharging us at midnight. But as soon as we were in bed it started again. I rang the sister who said 'sit him up and lean him forward and hold his nose, he mustn't talk or speak or it will start again.' We took it in turns to hold his nose as our arms grew tired, until it subsided at around 4.00 a.m. Throughout this Corin was stoical and brave. Sitting up against the pillows, not speaking, but smiling at my attempts to joke as we took turns to hold his nose.

> We are acting parts in a play that we have never read and never seen, whose plot we don't know, whose existence we can glimpse, but whose beginning and end are beyond our present imagination and conception.
>
> *Family Scenarios*, R.D. Laing

Cheek by Jowl used this quote in their notes for *The Tempest* and it seemed a fair description of our situation.

Dr Jim MacKeith came to visit us. A very close friend of ours, his mother 'Jo' was my mother's best friend since school days, and her daughter Alice is my oldest friend. Corin and he had worked on human rights issues together. Jim said to Corin, 'You must write every day in your notebook, it doesn't have to be 'meaningful' or clever, just simple facts, but you must write'.

Corin's diary
October 2005
The spy who came in from the cold

In my bedroom… well, not really my bedroom, more a spare room, but made to look sort of like my bedroom. A single bed, books, records, framed prints and photos on the walls. A married, twice-married man, who, nevertheless, in his imagination, is unmarried. Outside, autumn. John le Carré.

November, almost. Yet outside, in my garden, and in Greg and Barbara's, the leaves on the pear tree are still dark olive. Music. BB?

I watched a video film, taken in the US, of Vanessa, Lynn and Rachel doing a very moving performance in aid of Gregory Peck's institute. Watching the video at Vanessa's no one else present except she and I, was deeply moved. So little time had passed since I could sit *in* Vanessa's sitting room *with* Rachel.

I tried to explain this to Vanessa. She understood, I think. But although she was understanding, it was a difficult feeling. Not, in any way, Vanessa's fault. No fault attached. Just difficult. Time passing, however short, affects two people, both very close, differently. Somewhat.

[…]

Tonight, Sally [Simmons] comes by, for company. I'm terrifically fond of Sally. Her presence is very comforting. Though enough strange moods seem to intervene, even now.

6.55 p.m. Pitch dark outside.

I mentioned, when Sally came up to look at the room, my need for a larger more practical work table. 'So you could put the lamp on it' she suggested, quite rightly. (At present the table is so small, that the reading lamp sits on a little table beside the main table.)

At last, in November 2005, Corin began his rehabilitation at the Wolfson Neurorehabilitation Centre as an outpatient. These are the hasty fragments of notes that I took at the first sessions.

...One of Corin's great resources is his capacity to adapt to his environment (his skill as an actor) a real strength. Sometimes this covers up a level of confusion and people may think he's more in control than he is.

He has no capacity to reflect.

He is highly tuned to the emotional dynamic of the situation.

His skills are fine-tuned – and he *reacts* but may not understand why. He can feel patronised.

He is searching for grounding.

He can learn but he doesn't know he has learned it, and he can't access it.

His working memory is good.

He can cope in the moment.

All patients with brain injury have insight problems. His self-awareness has been damaged but improved insight can lead to depression…

In other words the more he understands, the more difficult and upsetting it will be for him.

We, the family are in trauma, he is not. In a way that is a helpful thing… Corin's adjustment will be led by the <u>family</u> adjustment…

These notes really describe the enormous challenges and difficulties that lay ahead. For a start, none of us had yet remotely adjusted to Corin's predicament. Sometimes I think I never fully understood the severity of his illness. We, the family, should be <u>leading</u> the adjustment, but I wasn't even on the first step.

Yet here are Corin's summaries of the first rehab sessions – and they gave so much hope to me and the family.

Friday 25 November 2005
Psychology session

I've been questioning why I am coming to the Wolfson, and we discussed this today in the session.

I am brought to an understanding and acceptance of the fact that damage has been done to my memory, and my knowledge of this has been strengthened by the realisation that it is hard for me to draw conscious memories of previous events. I've been doing certain radio plays, for instance, but I've been unable to recall actually being at the radio station.

I'm not rejecting that I *have done them*, because I've seen the evidence in my own handwriting. I need to be able to work with a system which I can trust in the same way that I have been always able to rely on my conscious recollection, which came as images to my mind, and therefore confirmed something was true.

But now I don't get those images, and so I need to find a new system in order to be able to find what is true. The system I am learning to rely upon involves my trusting my own handwriting. Learning to trust my handwriting as the mechanism for recalling knowledge and events is a challenge because I've always relied on images for these things. Now I must learn to look in my Filofax when I want to remember something. I've always been in control of my own life – but now, because of this memory problem I rely on other people to tell me what is there and what is not, and this frustrates me.

Wednesday 30 November 2005
Psychology session with Dr B

I recognise that it is difficult for me to remember conscious memories of what has happened. It makes me feel very 'at sea'. What are the implications of this? It feels very ominous. To be able to hold on to what has happened to me, and why. This is my goal to why I am at The Wolfson. To achieve this. It's about revisiting this information regularly, until it becomes familiar to my unconscious memory.

I'm not going to remember consciously what happened, but the hope is that I can hold this information as a knowledge that I can believe and trust.

Saturday 3 December 2005

I asked Kika what I was like before...?...? 'Have I been away?'

She replied, 'Yes, in a way because you've been so ill, but we're going to put everything back together like a jigsaw puzzle.'

OCTOBER 2005
Back to Work

Corin's diary 2005

Filming. Trying to work out where I was, what I was doing.
At times I felt like a man who has fallen overboard from an
immense liner.

In the midst of this totally changed and frightening environment, the
postman delivered the brown paper A4 envelope that actors long for. It
was a script for Corin.

Justin Hardy was making a film about the liberation of Belsen.
Knowing the situation with Corin, he nevertheless wanted him to play
the Major and Jemma to play a Red Cross nurse. For Jemma, who had
always wanted to work with her father but never had, it was a dream
come true. Arden went along with them to look after Corin and to be
an extra. A bright glow in the darkest of times.

Corin's diary
Sunday 29 October 2005

A lovely day! Our visitor… Mark Rylance! An absolutely
delightful man… We sat and talked for an hour in the front
room and then went to the nearby Cafe Méliès.

[undated] November 2005

Justin Hardy visited us.

Another lovely day.

Arden and Jemma with me… hooray!

Sunday 13 November 2005

Read-through of *The Belsen Redemption*.

Jemma has a good part. Arden a good job.

Monday 14 November 2005

A long day's work on the Belsen script. I just want to say what a great help and pleasure it is to be working with Arden! He has such a great spirit!

Kika's diary
Thursday 17 November 2005

Jehane came by to take me down to Mum's for the day, we were looking forward to a breakfast together but Corin wakes up confused, agitated, no heart attack, no letters, where are his clothes? Arden? Harvey? 'Look stop playing games and talk to me as Kika would you?' I can't go with Jehane, which I mind terribly. C gets dressed without washing. Even in hospital he always washed.

Corin and I made pesto together. C was nervous about doing it so I gave him the ingredients and he pounded away with the pestle. Results were pleasing. Corin was happier and the sauce was delicious. I made him a ravioli and went to get some fish and chips. 'Don't be long,' he says. He rings me the moment I'm out of the door.

Friday 18 November 2005

Corin goes to bed early and wants me to go with him. Says 'I love you, you are my one and only,' then 'Oh God, feel this lump'. I tell him it's a defibrillator and notice that there's a scar that I can show him next time he doesn't believe he's been in hospital or had a heart attack.

I must be strong for the boys and Corin. That must be my aim. But how?

And suddenly I got a part in a fascinating project, a BBC adaptation of *The Line of Beauty* by Alan Hollinghurst. At first I felt very shaky and overwhelmed by the other actors' kindness. Luckily I was playing Margaret Thatcher, which meant I had to be steely and formidable. Unbending as well as flirtatious, but above all not an ounce of doubt or uncertainty. Impossible in my predicament but in fact it was rather liberating. I couldn't have undertaken work without the help of our new carer Miranda, whose natural beauty, glamour and cheffing skills cheered us all up, especially Corin. She remained with us for about two years and has become a good friend.

Then came a new play at the Arcola, *Gaudeamus* by Peter Morris and directed by Michael Longhurst, a brilliant satire on an American college that got closed down for experimenting in free love in the Sixties. I played a sixty-year-old classics professor who is a virgin and decides to go along with the sexual experiment. It was a cast of three and our parts were monologues. I loved my part – it was all about sex and Socrates. But I suffered from bad stage fright – so awful that I could barely stand on stage. I had huge guilt that I was able to memorise lines and Corin was not. Unbearable. Corin's memory was legendary in the acting profession. Corin came to the first night and 'bravoed' at the end, always, always supporting.

And then, just when Corin was beginning to fret about the next job, as all actors do, and having to be reassured and reminded that he'd only just completed the work on the Belsen film, he got offered another great role. Beckett's *Krapp's Last Tape* for the radio. Polly Thomas (the director) said:

> …I hadn't known Corin before his stroke, and was unprepared for the sudden transformation. As he read, as he became Krapp, he unleashed great power and energy. It was extraordinary – in a simple setting, Beckett's brilliant, sly words were brought to life as if they had been written for Corin.

There were some film roles that Corin performed which was joyful for all of us although I will not divulge here how we got insurance. Another nightmare for people who have had a heart attack. Justin Hardy, Robin Soames, Stephen Poliakoff, and Polly Thomas, Ned Chaillet, and Nicholas Hytner are all directors that were willing to take the risk with Corin and I thank them for it profoundly.

In December we were lucky enough (through Tim Owen, my son-in-law, who knew him through his human rights work) to get a consultation with Professor Michael Kopelman, Head of the Neuropsychiatry and Memory Disorders Clinic and Professor of Neuropsychiatry at the Institute of Psychiatry, King's College, London.

Corin's diary

December 2005

This morning we saw Mike Kopelman at St Thomas's.

I like him. Seeing him and Kika with me gives me confidence.

Kopelman, or Mike as we came to know him, said that Corin needed intensive rehab, but that he wouldn't get it on the NHS, which was depressing. He also explained that there was so much more to be learned about brain injury than was in the textbooks and that essentially it is *time* that brings about change. Kopelman does not have a private practice. He is dedicated to the NHS, therefore his clinic is always full, sometimes oversubscribed. He was kind and wise and always helpful. It was a tremendous relief to know that he would see Corin regularly as his time at the Wolfson Clinic was coming to an end. Meanwhile I was starting to see an analyst to help me deal with the anxiety attacks and a kind of morbid depression which overwhelmed me at times.

Corin missed the intellectual excitement of academic life and was always trying to get Gabe, me, Alfie, and Jemma down to Cambridge, and I did go with him two or three times. We would walk along the Cam with family friend Marina Voikhanskaya. She would feed us home-grown tomatoes, cheese, red wine, and strawberries. Happy visits.

Years later we went to a lecture on memory given by Professor Kopelman at King's College in London. There was a north-east wind blowing, and hail, and we couldn't get a taxi. We arrived at the hall soaking wet. As soon as the lecture began Corin sat forward. He was completely engrossed as he is at the theatre, watching and listening with a sort of fierce detachment. By that I mean Corin was never someone you could nudge or whisper to in the middle of a performance. Oh how I wished I had thought of it before now. Taking him to a lecture, I mean.

Jim MacKeith's widow Keesje was at Kopelman's lecture with Gwen, their beautiful daughter, they were all friends. I write this today because one of the most moving experiences back in 2006 was when Kopelman came over to our place and listened with some friends to *Krapp's Last Tape* being broadcast. Corin was so happy. We toasted him with champagne. I liked the fact that they both got the chance to see and hear each other's work.

CHAPTER EIGHTEEN

2006

Holiday Breaks

Corin's diary

Wednesday 15 March 2006

A lovely visit from Jemma. We walked on Tooting Common and it gave me so much joy to be with her.

Corin keeps asking me when we're going to Paris. The thought of the Eurostar journey and the wine, was too daunting for now, so I ask him if he'd like to go to Cornwall and he's very pleased.

Cornwall 2006

Corin, Petra and I went to Zennor for three days. It was quite early on in Corin's illness and I hadn't travelled with him before, so Petra kindly came with me. On the way down Corin refused to observe the no smoking signs on the train, and kept disappearing into the loo for a quick smoke. Very soon loudspeakers announced that smoking on trains is forbidden, and anyone caught would be fined and put off the train. Then Transport Police started to patrol the corridors, following the smell of Benson & Hedges as it wafted down the corridor. Petra and I turned to stone and read our books intently each time they passed: we knew where Corin was. How he managed to avoid them we will never know, but he did, and got to Penzance without being caught. Corin wrote a short account.

Corin's diary

I had a lovely short (two days) holiday in Cornwall, staying
with Sue Wilson [the very nice owner of the B&B]. Two
women arrived yesterday morning, one of them Rachel
Kavanaugh, the artistic director at Birmingham Repertory.

I'm afraid I didn't stay to talk with them, but went down to
The Tinners Arms for a drink. Last night, we went to a lovely
hotel with a restaurant for dinner. I had a fish called ling!

A most enjoyable time. No swimming, though we did go
down to the sea.

Very Nice.

Petra's Poem

St Ives

Now we have reached the shoreline and the tide is going out –
The sand is stretched with little shells and seagulls shout –
You stood in shorts holding Kika's hand,
The sea was cold you had no plan
To swim and nor did we, we craved the crab
In spongy bread, and as we put it to our lips,
A seagull plunged and made a grab,
And took our lunch which frightened us to leave
And have ice cream beneath a brolly

You bought a card for Tom,

Then, loaded down with plastic bags,

We caught the bus, you bought some fags,

And suddenly, the sun was gone,

The fields in mist where once it shone.

Corin's holiday with Luke

Saturday 10 March 2006

With Luke – in Malta! We've just had a really marvellous
dinner – in Sliema!

Coming home – listening to beautiful classical stringed
music. Oh! Ah!

Sunday 11 March 2006

A peaceful night. Luke woke me with a cup of tea at 11.00 a.m.
One look out of the window convinced me that I wanted to
stay here for at least another week. One more week in Malta!
Aaah!!!

This morning we're heading for a restaurant highly praised in
the guidebook, specialising in rabbit! It's called 'Bobbyland',
and is to be found on Dingli Cliffs!!

Lunch, 2 p.m. on Dingli Cliffs

We're having lunch at the romantically (well… actually rather murderously named)

It fully persuaded me that rabbit is one of the most delicious dishes you can cook and eat.

Monday 12 March 2006

This heavenly morning began with a visit to beautiful Mdina. Once inside we found a delightful bar, and had a lager!! Haha!!

And then, a little later, Luke showed me an absolutely brilliant short film he had made… *Strangers*!!

CHAPTER NINETEEN

FEBRUARY 2007
Our Mother Dies

Corin's diary

February 2007

Kika went down on Friday to take Olive to hospital. Alone in London, I got up in the morning and made breakfast. Do it for Kika! Alone, I looked after myself. Encouraging!

Mum is getting noticeably more frail with each week that passes. She's looking forward to meeting up with my dad again, although she's not sure where that would be. When she was younger and fitter, her grief over his death was profound. I tried hard to help her. I wanted her to feel better. I tried to 'argue' her into cheering up... and if that failed I would write lists of things that she could do when feeling blue.

I would scold her for saying how lonely she was, didn't she know she had her daughters? I would shake my head in frustration when she would say finally 'it's just not having him to talk to at night...' I understand now Mum.

Mum was brave. Deported from Germany in the 1930s, she was later arrested with my father in the Soviet Union for distributing leaflets for the Campaign Against Abuse of Psychiatry. When told by the KGB to strip in the prison cell, she famously replied that she had never minded taking her clothes off.

She felt like a stranger to me at times, yet a stranger I knew better than anyone else in the world. Has she left me finally? I think not. Five years after her death, struggling into my Lois Selfridge black Edwardian dress, I caught sight of myself. My mother stared straight back at me. It seems I have also inherited her furrowed brow, anxiousness, a secret 'showing off' look and heavy Jewish eyelids. My mother is Jewish, so therefore I am, but I grew up unaware of it as my parents were against all religions, and I was ignorant of all faiths. All that I know about the Bible was taught to me by Corin.

She wrote a story about me called 'The Green Veil'. It was about a little girl, Erika Sarah Louise (my name), who was afraid to walk the one-and-a-half miles to school (which I was) because some boys used to lie in wait for her and threaten to put her in their cooking pot – so the hedge that grew along the lane, and that had become her confidante, told her a story to distract her until she reached the school. It is a charming story, which I treasure, and look forward to reading to my grandchildren.

Later, when I was sent to weekly boarding school at seven years old, Sundays were coloured with the dread of going back. Even now, waving goodbye to a close friend, sister or any of my children brings on an embarrassing rush of tears.

Kika's diary

February 2007

'I'm waving goodbye to you!' Mum announced as my sisters and I arrived at her bedside in the hospital. She has, of course, been preparing us for her death for at least twenty years, much as one would warn a small child that a pet has a limited life. She carried her will in her handbag and would provocatively wave it in the air… 'See, I'm prepared,' she would say to shocked visitors. 'I've lived too long. Even the trees are telling me that.'

That night someone had brushed her hair the wrong way and her skin was yellow and white. My heart lurched. 'You look better,' I lied. 'I've been very worried about you... and upset'. 'Oh really, Kika, I haven't shed a tear'. She looks, horrified and fascinated, as a very old lady with long hair scraped back, no teeth and stick legs, clambers very slowly on to the bed next to hers. 'Is that me? Is it a mirror? How's Corin?'

My eyes fill up. I look away.

'Oh it's a mess,' she sighs.

On an earlier visit, after settling her down with the *Guardian* crossword, I headed for the exit, but suddenly I was overcome by an ancient grief and ran back to hug her. She looked up, pleased. 'Why did you come back?' in a roguish tone.

'Because I missed you. Bye Mum.'

On the train going back to London I thought about her 'Why did you come back?' Did she mean 'do you really love me then?' or 'why did you bother...?'

An old theme.

My mother is now in a nursing home. We drive down to
see her. Corin and I sing 'Oxygen' to the tune of Edelweiss.
'Oxygen, oxygen, left my brain in a hurry / Oxygen, oxygen,
come back soon or I'll wor--ry.'

Sunday 4 March 2007

At the nursing home Mum is sleeping, chin on hand, sitting
in the chair by the window. Corin, Christina – our kind
Italian friend who had once looked after Mum – and I wait
a little in the 'waiting area'. I go in alone and kneel down by
her chair. 'Mummy.' Her eyes open wide and see nothing.
Morphine. Then they see me and soften. She seems to glow.
She folds her arms round me and kisses me softly over and
over. It's more than a hug, it's comfort and need and love, and
I want it to last forever. It's all there is to do really, the rest is
filling in time.

'What's the theatre news?'

'We're not in a play right now, Mum.'

'Look at the colours.' She points to the red, yellow and purple
tulips on the window sill.

She reads Arden's latest poem very slowly and carefully with a magnifying glass. Corin's making a beeline for the bed, lies down and has a nap. She closes her eyes in the chair. I sit between them. 'Comb my hair,' she murmurs.

'You are so beautiful Olive,' says Corin, waking up. She smiles, pleased, but with the old disbelieving, ironic smile.

Friday 9 March 2007

Peaceful scene. Mum is tucking into fried egg, bacon, fried potatoes, beans, with quiet enjoyment. Sitting next to the window.

I don't disturb her.

She says later, 'I am happy here.'

And

'I'm alright here. You can leave me here and go and be happy together.' To Petra and me.

Petra and I go outside to the car. Petra is very upset.

Wednesday 21 March 2007

I got up and saw there were lots of missed calls on the mobile. I rang Jehane. She sounded normal. I was relieved. 'I thought something must have happened.' Her voice changed.

'You don't know?'

'Oh God, Mum, did she die?'

'Oh Kika, yes…'

It was the first day of spring. The same day, though not year, as Michael Redgrave had died: 21st March.

Kika's diary

Wednesday 21 March 2007

We meet at the Llama Park coffee shop. White faced, pink eyed. We went to see Mum. She was lying too straight on her back, hair back on the pillow. Mouth a bit askew, one eye a little open, still focusing. I kissed her forehead. So cold and damp. An unnatural cold I'd never felt before. From the bottom of a deep black lake. She didn't look peaceful or unhappy but enigmatic and like a Rembrandt painting of a death mask.

'Her skin's going waxy,' Sonie says. 'Do you have to use that word?' I say. 'What's wrong with waxy?'

We busy ourselves in the small room packing her clothes. That wasn't so bad, but seeing her spotted red hankies was.

What a silence in the room. I got acquainted with death. I became a little less frightened. I worried about her hands and arms. Too straight under the heavy counterpane, I stroked them and rearranged them to be more comfy.

Bon Voyage

Oh Mother, you have gone

Down the dark corridor

Where rose pink worms live.

We sit round like sacked staff

Chewing the cud,

Railing against your impossible conditions.

All the gifts that we brought you

Still cannot compensate

For the loss we are about to inherit.

You sailed away on a cloud

Of morphine and flowers and love.

We hope, we almost pray.

Jehane Markham
May 2007

The inability to control events began to disable me. Corin's recovery was stagnant. There were only good days and bad days. My sisters were intent on selling the cottage only four weeks after our mother's death. Apparently I had been the one to suggest 'upmarket' estate agents. Our voices cracked at one another. Could it be that after her death we would grow apart? We ached for our Mum.

Thursday 19 April 2007

Joely and Daisy sent a wonderful bunch of multi-coloured roses. Petra came and brought a box of ripe mangoes. I felt better. Besides the real world was galloping on with arrangements for Harvey and Jodie's wedding day. Menus, placemats, flowers, guests, the DRESS, the present list…

On 27 May the Great Day finally came. We travelled down to Chilham where Jodie's parents lived: Tom and Jacquie Reed – we always had fun staying with them and Corin was particularly impressed that they lived opposite a pub. Jodie and Harvey had been married formally at Islington Town Hall and now they were going to have a humanist ceremony. My school friend, Suzannah Stack, was the Registrar for both ceremonies, which made it even more special. In Chilham it poured with rain, so the entire wedding had to take place in a little village school, under wooden eaves. Jodie and Harvey had written their own vows, beautiful and romantic. Later, under the marquee, Corin recited 'Shall I compare thee to a summer's day?' to them, Tom Brind, the best man, gave a wonderful speech, and I sang 'Our love is here to stay'.

CHAPTER TWENTY

AUGUST 2007
No Future?

Kika's diary

August 2007

We were listening to *King Lear* on Radio 3, Corin playing Lear and me Regan. Corin looking puzzled. He shook his head. 'Who's written this? It's not Shakespeare' (although earlier he'd said 'I did this before Stratford').

It was distressing. Well I was sad, he didn't seem to be. 'It's normal,' he said.

'Yes, it's normal,' I agreed.

'Thank you, you're so helpful,' he said.

He just didn't recognise any of the text that he heard. I found his old copy of the play and he read it for a bit and said he thought it was a little more familiar, but that he wasn't convinced. We continued listening to the play.

'Who's written it?' he asked when it ended.

One of the few pictures Corin ever took of me at Nelson Bay, South Island.

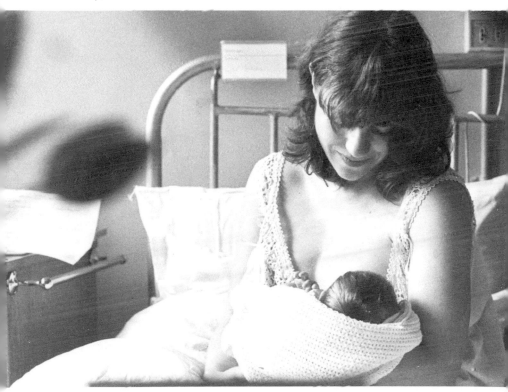

3 February 1979. Harvey at three days old.

Our wedding day, 5 October 1985

On holiday in Belagio. I was telling them to enjoy
the view but they all insisted on looking tragic.

Jemma and Luke with their dad in New York.

Left: Harvey in full Arsenal kit.
Right: Arden with pig bat in our field adjacent to Lear Cottage.

The company of Moving Theatre at Chelsea Theatre, World's End.

At our favourite café in Jardin du Luxembourg.

Corin as Oscar in *De Profundis*.

Corin's first visit to Lear Cottage since his heart attack.

At a rally in Trafalgar Square against the bombing of Gaza. January 2009.

Corin and Jemma at the Globe after seeing *Pericles*, the production he was in when he was taken ill. Going back was emotional. The audience gave him a standing ovation.

Reading the names of the dead in 'Voices of the Lebanon' in Trafalgar Square with Simon Callow and Bill Patterson.

Arden's graduation day – a moment of triumph!

Corin holds Edie, four days old.

Corin at peace in Jehane and Roger's garden in Norfolk.

Jodie and Harvey and Edie Redgrave a couple of weeks after Corin's death coming back from the Isle of Wight on the ferry. We decided to go there for a weekend, to stay at the Royal Hotel, where Corin and I had many a happy weekend.

Corin stands in the garden. He has just peed there. He holds his hand strangely behind his back and I realise it's because he is holding a cigarette.

'I won't smoke any more. This will be my last.' He sees I'm crying. He gives me the cigarettes.

I go back to the computer to finish off an email. An awful cry comes from the garden. Corin is sitting at the table (still smoking) and his chair is giving way slowly under him.

'Hold me! Hold me up!' As he's only six inches from the ground and very heavy, I'm finding it difficult.

'Just sit down, I've got you.'

'No, don't let go of me, GET ME UP!' he yells. Amazingly I manage to get him to his feet, still with the cigarette. I cry on the telephone and Hyu Jong, Arden's girlfriend, holds me tightly, 'Shush, no, Kika, Kika don't cry.' I gently detach her and tell her it's making me worse.

Meanwhile, Corin has been to the shops and brought back a bottle of champagne, which he opens and we all dutifully drink.

Later he explains that when he falls he feels as if there is no ground, only space.

Corin continued to get intermittent work – after *Krapp's Last Tape* he recorded another radio play *Life After Scandal*, by Robin Soans, playing Jonathan Aitken, the disgraced Tory MP, brilliantly. He went to Sheffield with Jemma for a workshop on Pinter, playing the part of Hirst, a distinguished poet, in *No Man's Land*, which he'd done at the National before his heart attack.

But it was in 2007, in the summer after my mother's death, that Corin and I had a very painful, truthful conversation. We were facing up to the fact that we had come to *hate* the roles we had become used to playing: Corin in the role that constantly needed to be 'monitored', me the monitor, forever on the lookout for a misdemeanour. That he was becoming a scapegoat for everything. All my disappointments. No wonder he was turning to drink, I thought. He was due to go to Stratford-upon-Avon to a poetry recital to read the poems of Louis MacNeice and W.H. Auden the following day, and began to get very emotional. 'I am very depressed. You don't know how near I am to the lid coming down. I HAVE NO FUTURE!'

This cry from the heart was deeply upsetting.

I had to answer him as carefully as I could: 'Your life may not be the same as it was, or you would like it to be, but you do have a future. You have proved you can work professionally, so much so that you're going to play Tynan again in New York. Your creative power has not diminished one bit. You can write about how it feels to be an actor who has lost his memory. You've been wanting to do that for months. You almost died, but you came back. You mustn't waste this chance.'

The fact is there were parts offered from time to time but sometimes the director or producer didn't know that Corin had a heart attack or its effects on him. Together Helen and Lisa, Corin's excellent agents from Feast Management, and I had to make the difficult decision as to what Corin could manage to do. We would discuss the role together. How many lines were there? How much stamina would he need? Would the fact that he was working be so enjoyable to him that he would overcome any risk he might encounter emotionally and mentally?

In the end I had to make the decision. A few times Lisa and I would have to turn down work as it would be too physically demanding for him. Saying no to work on my husband's behalf and not telling him was nothing less than an unspeakable crime. That's how it felt. Terrible.

So I show him the email that Vanessa has just sent with all the details of *Tynan* in New York, as I know he thinks that I'm just trying to keep him happy. He cheers up and we kiss. He helps me lay the table, and goes to the shop to get sparkling water and bread.

His high spirits last, and the next day he gets up early and bravely goes off to Stratford for the recital. I join him later. His reading is beautiful. Every word counted. At the end he left the last poem hanging in the air, looking into the audience with an expression of defiance and acute sadness. Huge applause. Azmat Begg, Vivian and John Blizzard, his dresser from Stratford (whom he adored), were there. He didn't ask for a drink. On the way back he could feel the memory of the recital fading. He was conscious of it going, like a receding dream. The next morning I was looking for the nail scissors, as usual they were never where they should be. 'I don't suppose you've seen them?' I wasn't expecting an answer. 'Actually, I think you'll find them in the fruit bowl in the kitchen. I saw them there a week ago.' He was right! They were!

That summer Corin flew to New York, accompanied by Malcolm Tierney, to work with Richard Nelson on *Tynan*, staying with his sisters at Lynn's home in the country. Richard and Corin had always loved working together. On 22 October, 2007, Corin gave a spectacular reading of *Tynan* at the Public Theatre. The audience was spellbound. Many of them didn't know he was ill. How did Richard enable Corin to do this? I think Corin had always trusted him as a director and now he had to trust him with his illness. Richard never patronised him, he wanted the best from Corin and Corin responded.

The next year Richard worked with Corin on *De Profundis* by Oscar Wilde.

Corin performed the monologue at the National Theatre. It was both funny and heartbreaking. Corin's tears were real, but it was Oscar you saw, weeping in prison. Trevor Nunn said it made him realise what a wonderful thing a 'reading' was, because it allowed the actors to be completely in the moment. At the end, the entire audience stood as one person, clapping and crying in recognition not just for his performance but his bravery.

Corin's diary:

A wonderful evening at the National Theatre. The first performance [of the last two] at the Lyttelton Theatre.

A really heart-warming reception (in fact a standing ovation!) at the end.

Then we went upstairs to the Green Room. Darling Kika, dear Vivian and I. A lovely gathering of friends. Francis Wyndham, Peter Eyre, and… Ian Bostridge! He has invited me to do an evening with him at the Barbican in October.

Lovely dinner in the Mezzanine. I'm afraid I drank too much. I am promising myself (and everybody else) not to do that tonight!

Oh… a wonderful evening, though!

CHAPTER TWENTY-ONE

MARCH 2008

AA

Kika's diary

Saturday 8 March 2008

Corin is becoming eccentric. He stops people in the street to talk to them. Children. Women with pushchairs or prams.

Today he saw a sleeping baby in a buggy and talked to an older woman.

'You're the mother?'

'No.'

'Well it's a lovely baby.'

'I'm just the...' But Arden and I didn't hear any more, we were getting embarrassed and waited to move him on to Café Méliès. After more chat, as we move off: 'Well can I just kiss your hand?' He kisses her hand Old Jolyon-style, very gracefully.

'How charming!' she cries.

Arden and I exchange a look. Perhaps we're being too stuffy. After all some people seem to like being accosted by Corin in the street.

It's Sunday 21st and I've missed all the business with the Waitrose man. I don't know what this means, but it seems profound. Kika says that I overheard a customer saying very racist remarks to a black security man. I became angry and told him that I'd heard everything and that he was to leave the premises immediately.

'Fuck off out of it!'

I was much applauded by the staff at Waitrose.

Summer Time. Alcoholic Days and Nights.

Corin spends the evening with our friend Peter Marsden, author of a book on the Taliban and former aid worker in Afghanistan. Unfortunately, Peter's experience of working with the Taliban was of no help when it came to persuading Corin not to drink. So I arrive back to find Corin extremely drunk. Peter leaves. Suddenly Corin heads off upstairs to get to the lavatory but doesn't make it in time. We swear at each other, me in fury, he in misery, and I begin to scrub the carpet, shoes, socks etc., anywhere the unseemly evidence has landed. I try to persuade Corin to get into the shower, but he won't. He takes off his clothes – but wants to have another cigarette first, and goes into the garden and sits down at the old table under the tree.

From the kitchen door I can see his white back and bottom looming at me as he stubbornly puffs away. I want to giggle. I am holding a bowl and rubber gloves, and he is naked on a garden chair at midnight.

When the children were little, Corin used to make up stories for them at bedtime. Their favourite was always 'The Big Bad Monkey'. The Big Bad Monkey was the king of the jungle and was a terrible show-off. He played mean tricks on the other animals, who would finally rebel and make traps for him where he would fall into piles of shit and be very humiliated. There would be shrieks of laughter coming down the stairs and I would try and listen, but it was strictly a boy thing between the three of them.

When Corin got ill he sometimes seemed to delight in inhabiting the Big Bad Monkey. One of the most difficult things for me to handle was the disinhibition factor, which meant he could make very graphic physical passes at women, friends, relations, friends of relations. I knew he couldn't help it, but each time there was an incident, I felt bitterly hurt and would weep and remonstrate, and he would be puzzled and sorry.

Disinhibition also happened over peeing. He started to pee in the garden, not discreetly, and if he thought no one was around would piss straight out of the kitchen door. I tried every tactic possible to persuade him not to do this, sometimes in tears, sometimes in anger, and sometimes sweetly, but nothing worked. One day when we were both together in the kitchen, I pulled down my trousers and pants and squatted on the doorstep. Corin looked at me in amazement. 'Darling, what on earth are you doing?'

'I thought I'd have a pee. What's wrong? You do it all the time.' 'Well I will NEVER do it again!'

He looked horrified. It was a risky strategy, but it worked and I felt incredibly proud.

Kika's diary
Wednesday 23 July 2008

Corin has agreed to try AA. As it happens, the meeting place is round the corner from where we live. Corin and I arrive an hour early and sit on a bench in the little front yard. At 7.30 some men arrive, and an Irish man with thick, grey, curly hair and a comforting voice introduces himself, shakes Corin's hand and says 'You've done the right thing coming here. I'll make you a cup of tea'. He goes off with Corin.

I feel as though I'm leaving one of the children behind at the first day of school, and then I realise that it was indeed the building used by Harvey's first pre-nursery school! Later Corin comes back; he stayed for the whole meeting and was impressed by the ordinary blokes and the honesty and friendliness. Euphoria.

AA

Sunday 3 August 2008

Corin is nearly mugged by a West Indian couple, a man and woman. They came to our local restaurant, Caminata, where he was having a drink with a neighbour, and refused to go away and tried to take his wallet. A guardian angel in the shape of a six-foot black man appeared, saying he was police and unless they went away he would arrest them. This did the trick and they melted away. I have tried to find out where he lived, but to no avail. He too melted away, so I haven't been able to thank him yet.

Saturday 9 August 2008

I talk Corin into going to the Saturday AA meeting at 10 a.m., and go with him as far as the gate. There are already some men chatting on the steps. They look very kind. 'Is this right for the AA?' I only ask because they were waiting at a different entrance.

They nod.

'Don't worry, we'll look after him.' And they do. Afterwards Corin says, 'I feel in the right place.' 'Do you feel you have something in common?' 'Yes.'

We hedge around it. It seems that he can acknowledge that he has a 'small' drink problem. (To *me*, not to the group.)

I've been to Al-Anon, the organization that AA runs to help friends' members living with alcoholics. Now I realise I shouldn't say the word 'alcoholic' – he may or may not come to acknowledge it but unless it comes from him it won't count. Looking at the leaflet of Al-Anon, *You and Alcoholism*, I realize I'm displaying every symptom of co-dependency – including rage. I haven't yet committed any violence though...

As Corin's recovery continued, I feel able to go to France for a few days that summer, while Corin goes to stay with Jemma in Wales.

Kika's diary
Wales, Thursday 28 August 2008

I am on the train to Stansted. I have done it! Packed for Corin who is on the train to Wales, packed for myself. We are going to separate holidays like Anne and Claude in *Anne and Muriel*. I phone Corin from my train and at first he doesn't answer, and I fear that he's gone to the bar already or is smoking in the corridor. It has taken four years for Corin to be able to travel on his own on the tube but he has never travelled on a journey like this unaccompanied. Jemma had wanted someone to travel with him but no one was available, besides both Corin and I felt confident that he could manage it. He hadn't been drinking for a week and although we were taking a risk, yes, because he could get off at the wrong

station, become ill on the train, get caught smoking in a
loo, I felt he would be OK if he could remember to keep his
mobile on so Jemma and I could ring him. The fact that the
mobile was ringing was a tremendous relief – the fact that he
wasn't answering was not! Meanwhile I rattled along past the
sleepy barges and tumbled willow lakes and canals of the Lea
Valley which shine out among the ugly suburbs and factories
that accompany one on the journey from Liverpool Street
to Stansted. I tried to ring him every ten minutes, with no
success.

Suddenly he answered. 'Hellooo?' 'Darling! Thank goodness!
Where were you?'

'Asleep!'

'I never thought of that. Have you got your sandwich?' 'I've
eaten it.'

'What, but that was meant for a mid-morning snack.'

'Well I've eaten it, it was lovely.'

He sounded very cheerful and together. I began to breathe
more easily.

'Leave it to the higher powers,' my Al-Anon group had said
and they were being proved right. In the departure lounge I
rang again and he was in the car with Jemma speeding up the
motorway to the Black Mountains. I felt calm and happy for
the first time.

At Bergerac, Sonie and Ernest are there to meet me, Sonie looking brown and beautiful in a blue and white dress. We drive though the luscious green countryside of the Dordogne Valley. Flowers of orange, purple, and crimson hang over the garden walls. The Vézère sparkled and lazed along under the bridges. Up the hill, through the meadows full of daisies till we arrive at La Melonie, the house with the blue doors and green shutters, bought by my father and mother back in the Sixties and now looked after by S and E. From the table under the tree we can see a red squirrel making its way down a branch. Hornets zoom about but seem more curious than hungry. As we sit down for a spread of melon, figs from the tree, cheese, stuffed courgettes and local wine, I glance at my mobile. Two messages are waiting. Both are from Jemma in an urgent voice asking me to ring her. The second one asking me to ring her as soon as possible. She hasn't said that Corin's ill so I'm trying not to be frightened when I call. The story is that Corin has somehow picked up the wrong case off the train and has thus lost all his clothes, his notebook with notes from Dr B's session, his script for the BBC *Turn of the Screw*, and worst of all his medication. They have only just discovered this, three hours after arriving in Wales and it's Bank Holiday with no chance of finding out anything until the following day when the bag might be returned to Bristol…

Never in all my days of anxiety and dread about going away and what could happen, could I have dreamt up such a scenario. Ever resourceful, Jemma rang our doctor, found out what the medication was and managed to get the local chemist to give her enough for the weekend. Corin managed to buy a new pair of trousers, and I eventually collected the lost bag from Crewe station.

Corin's diary

August 2008

I've been staying in Wales for a week, with Jemma and Tim and their boys, Alfie and Gabe. In the evenings I read 'The Rime of the Ancient Mariner'. They seemed immensely moved by the Coleridge, and I felt wonderfully rewarded by their response.

Kiku's Diary

Saturday 11 October 2008

I can say that in the three and a half years that followed this catastrophe, I have learned much from the events that unfolded; the compassion shown by the kind souls of Balham, shopkeepers and publicans as well as friends and neighbours. The creativity that endures despite the huge losses that occur is extraordinary. In brain injury I learned:

That there *are no* answers. But they may emerge.

The art of waiting/'Things can change after lunch'. The art of forgiving yourself.

That you *will* learn to take command of the situation and that very often you *do* know best…

A week at the Bush and 'Louise'

I'm working on *Bufonidae*, a one-woman play by Bryony Lavery, which had been commissioned by the Bush Theatre.

Kika's diary
Wednesday 15 October 2008

Dress rehearsal and first night. Horrible fear which I'm trying to combat.

My mobile rings in the dressing room. A message from our friend Bill Bingham, saying he's had a great afternoon with Corin and has left him in the capable hands of Louise.

Louise…??!! What? Who?

All kinds of images assail me, Louise massaging him and giving him a blow job in the sitting room.

Patricia, our temporary carer, is the next to ring, 'He's gone out with this woman and they've gone to the cashpoint, I'm trying to follow them…'

I walk down the Goldhawk Road, script in one hand, mobile in the other. I can't remember any text at all. I can only think of a young woman who is about to rob Corin, or seduce him.

I dry very badly in the dress rehearsal but get through the first night without a prompt. After the show I go to the Polish restaurant with Josie O'Rourke, Artistic Director at the Bush, and her parents. I am happy. We never find out who Louise was and what actually happened, although Corin had drawn out £100 but had nothing the next day. I'm sure he picked her up in a pub and asked her round. He seemed unsure who she was, when asked, except that she might have been collecting for a jumble sale. She hasn't turned up since. Although I'm rather hoping she will. I'm looking forward to hearing her story.

Kika's diary

Sunday 19 October 2008

We walk to the bookshop. When we go for a walk, Corin often walks on the opposite pavement. He doesn't come into the shop and has a coffee outside on the way back. He doesn't want to talk.

'You aren't enjoying this are you?'

'Yes, yes, it's lovely darling.'

He is polite and smiling. Walking quite fast for him. Never complaining. Locked away. Locked away from me with his placating smile and affectionate words. All I can do is hold his hand, which is warm and comforting. We shuffle through the pile of yellow and red sycamore leaves, along the path.

Kika's diary

Saturday 25 October 2008

Vanessa gives a radiant last performance [in the Joan Didion play, *The Year of Magical Thinking*, at the National Theatre]. We all manage to get lost going back to her dressing room. When we get there, Carlo, Vanessa's son, is offering sweet fairy cakes made by Lily and Jenny, his daughter and wife. Everyone else in the group has a wheat allergy and can't eat them. So, being helpful, Corin and I end up eating them all.

CHAPTER TWENTY-TWO

MARCH 2009
Going On

Corin's diary

Sunday 22 February 2009

Jemma came for lunch and I showed her the winnings I received from last night's bet. (Arsenal beat Milan i.e. £200.)

Kika said I had a fall in the kitchen.

Corin's diary:

Friday 6 March 2009

I have just woken up at 3 p.m. I decided to come downstairs and write a diary saying that, as usual, I had no idea of what I had done in the morning, what I had earlier for lunch, whether I had read the paper etc., etc. That would have been normal. But the situation was sharper than that. I discovered that I have a public performance, of a play called *The Trainer*. It is co-written by composer Keith Burstein whom I have met, and therefore know. A little. But a public performance! A reading, I assume. I, for certain, don't know any of my parts, lines. I am to wear a suit, I am told, and shall have to wash my hair.

Corin had forgotten that he had in fact produced Keith's opera, *Manifest Destiny*, years earlier. The reading went very well, performed by a brilliant cast: Tim Piggott-Smith, Janie Dee, Roger Lloyd-Pack and Corin.

We needed the sense of 'going on'. Corin and I were both locked in separate sorrowful worlds. Petra had observed one day that nature had not left Corin with anguish, but there was no certainty of that. I was still afraid of opening up a possible sorrow that I might not be able to contain or help him with. In a way we both understood that we couldn't risk damaging each other. We lived another sort of life, on a simpler level and kinder, with less expectation. I was struck by something Mark Thomas said about his father in a radio interview; 'we were learning to live with what we have of one another'. My analysis was strengthening me. I was getting better at dealing with my sorrow, rage and self-pity, able to be kinder to myself and that meant I was able to be kinder to Corin. Theatre was our consolation. The expression 'Doctor Theatre', a phrase used by all actors when ill, was never so true.

Every time we sat down and waited for a play to begin we were living in the moment waiting only for the next moment with anticipation, free of dread, and EQUAL. There was something else that gave us peace and contentment: *driving*. 'Ignore him…,' 'Pull over a bit more…,' 'Push on a bit…,' 'Bastard, don't give in to him…'. Such familiar comments were not onerous but comforting. I loved them. Whenever we drove it was as if nothing had ever happened.

A week after Corin came home, we started to be politically active again. The first event we took part in, was a vigil outside Stockwell tube station for Jean Charles de Menezes, the Brazilian electrician who'd been shot dead in the tube by the police in a botched case of mistaken identity. During the next four years we tried to attend any meetings for Shaker Aamer, still in Guantanamo and now extremely ill having been tortured.

We did readings in Trafalgar Square for 'Voices of Lebanon and Palestine' protesting against the Israeli attacks on Lebanon and Gaza and 'Naming the Dead', reciting the names of British soldiers and Afghan civilians killed in the first ten years of the war in Afghanistan.

Corin's diary

Saturday 28 March 2009

We took part in a rally in Trafalgar Square.

I read Robert Fisk.

We stood together on the platform – Kika read the diary of Zena el Khalil.

It was an honour to take part in such a dire, dreadful situation. It was important to feel that we could contribute, even in a small way.

We met Harvey and Jodie which was delightful. And Arden was there, dear Arden.

There was a Tamil hunger strike in Parliament Square. They were protesting against the wholesale slaughter that was being carried out by the Sri Lankan government against them. We went there and found the hunger striker lying in a tent. Corin managed to crawl on all fours through the tent flap to shake the man's hand, turn around and crawl back.

Apparently the protest is there every day. Simon Hughes, Lib Dem MP has been to visit the protest, but no other MP, so far as we heard.

I thought we should organise a meeting and get some well-known speakers to come.

In 2009, Corin reprised the part of Dalton Trumbo in the play *Trumbo*, with Nick Waring as Dalton's son. They had worked together before as Wilde and Bosie and laughed a lot. Corin loved Nick. John Dove directed them again for the Jermyn Street Theatre in London and at the Octagon in Bolton.

In March 2009 Corin's niece, Natasha Richardson died in a skiing accident. All the West End theatres dimmed their lights and Corin, who hadn't written anything down, came forward at the end of the play and spoke with great feeling and delicacy about how he remembered Natasha playing Ophelia, and that he'd taken Michael, his father, to see her performance, and that he loved her very much.

A visit to Tuscany.

Vanessa invites me out to where she and Franco (Nero) are making a movie on location in Tuscany for the weekend. San Quirico d'Orcia seems as hot as Africa and very beautiful. Vanessa and Franco make a very handsome couple. As they

walk down the high street holding hands, people smile and
wave and call out, 'Franco!' Walking behind them, I feel like
their governess. It is Sunday and Vanessa wants to light some
candles for Tasha. We go into the little eleventh-century
Chiesa di Santa Maria Assunta. No bigger than a cool, dark
high-ceilinged room. Four wooden pews on either side and
a little aisle in the middle. Vanessa sits on the second pew at
one end and I sit at the other. Franco lights some candles and
then sits between us. We are silent. The quiet around us is
gentle. Some tourists wander in and go out again. They don't
disturb us.

Gradually we become enveloped in an intense sorrow. An
outpouring of grief. Vanessa cries quietly with each breath
and I cry too. We choke and sniff and weep and wipe the
snot with our hands, no one seems to have any tissues. After
a bit Franco says softly 'Andiamo' to Vanessa. She gets up and
lights more candles and, after a bit, I light some with her.

We notice people have left notes to their loved ones pinned to
the wall and want to write one too.

> *Thank you darling Tash, for all the love you gave, Mum xxx*

> *Dearest Tasha, you are in our hearts and minds every day.
> All my love, Kika x*

Franco writes in Italian.

We put it on the picture, but it doesn't look very safe as there are no pins. Vanessa finds a little packet of tissues and we blow our noses. I put my arms around her and we stand like that for a minute. Then we go out into the blazing sun, but passing a stationery shop we dive in and Franco manages to get hold of a piece of Sellotape which he takes back to the church to fix Tasha's note more firmly to the wall. He takes Vanessa's hand and we walk back down the street.

CHAPTER TWENTY-THREE

2009

Memories

Corin's diary:

Friday 12 June 2009

I bought a packet of cigarettes, Rothmans, which upset Kika terribly. We both gave up smoking 14 years ago. But I told her, for comfort, that I wasn't intending to take it up again, only to take a step on – to do some bad things now and then!

Corin's diary

Friday 16 June 2009

Lying in bed is not necessarily tiredness, but finding a way to start the day. Arden told us some wonderful news. He got a 2:2 for his degree!! BRAVO ARDEN!!!! It hasn't been easy for him, with me being ill, and with him changing course in mid-stream. Tony Kushner came to supper. We talked a lot about writing.

Despite a great deal more exercise and a new, friendly carer – an aspiring writer, Alec Feest – and an analyst, Corin's health was deteriorating. We had been seeing Mike Kopelman with his colleague Liz Scott regularly, and together they would diplomatically but harshly challenge Corin over his drinking habits, and Mike had remarked in our last session that 'Corin is drinking himself to death'. The only person in the world who could now help him was Dr B, but she couldn't see him on the NHS. His allotted time was over, it would have to be private. I talked things over with Vanessa, and once again she came to our rescue and offered to pay for more sessions with Dr B.

These sessions were very significant and helped Corin greatly, both mentally and emotionally. But physically, he was deteriorating as he continued to smoke and drink.

We tried giving him non-alcoholic wine as (at first) he didn't seem to know the difference. It meant that I didn't have to nag him to have 'just one glass' all the time, but complicated things greatly if we were at an occasion where there was only real wine. I thought I should tell him the truth, that he was drinking sugared water, but the majority of the family thought otherwise and in the end Corin recovered enough to be able to tell the difference and wouldn't touch the non-alcoholic stuff!

One of the most painful and addictive habits, is thinking about our previous life. It's like picking a scab: you know it will bleed so you shouldn't, but you can't help it. The Old Life… Our flat in Paris; deciding which restaurant to try; what to eat; travelling on Eurostar together; acting together; making love; talking… talking, just talking; cooking; someone to put a plaster on your finger; to come to a hospital visit with you… Someone that leaves you beautifully written notes about shopping:

Darling,

I've gone to get some
Cat Food and Parmesan

back soon

C xxx

'*I've* had cancer!' says Corin.

We are on our way to Dr B's on a terrible cold night, through the dark turrets of Wimbledon. We are listening to Radio 4, to an account of the latest breakthrough in cancer research.

'Yes I know, I was with you at St George's Hospital when Roger [Kirby] diagnosed it. Do you remember?'

'No I don't.'

'How do you know you've had it then?' 'I'm not sure, I just do.' 'Do you remember the French restaurant we used to go to after your radiotherapy? And kind, elegant Miss Eyles? Our oncologist?'

'No, but do let's go to the restaurant next week. Perhaps I would remember it then.' Quite…

Inside the Wolfson in the reception area a man in a wheelchair was greeting strangers.

'Hello, are you a patient or a visitor?' he asks Corin. 'A visitor,' answers Corin.

OK, I think. I'm going to battle over this.

For once I begin the session by putting forward the idea that the reason Corin doesn't like coming to see Dr B is because it makes him feel there's 'something wrong with him' – that he doesn't believe that he's 'in recovery' because he doesn't think there's anything the matter.

A further exchange with Dr B shows that he's not sure he's even got a memory problem. I remind him that he didn't remember anything about his cancer, coming out of *The Cherry Orchard*, our holiday in Sweden afterwards, the hatred of the drugs he had to take.

'Oh yes, that's true...'

And then Dr B reminds him how, when she first treated him four years ago, he refused to believe he'd had a heart attack and how angry that made him because, as he couldn't remember having one, he thought people were lying to him and that his life was in danger, which was what led to his psychotic behaviour. It was only when she showed him reports on the internet of the call to the ambulance from Basildon Hall, the accounts in the papers, after weeks and weeks of going over similar material he gradually learned that perhaps it was true that he really had had a heart attack.

It became clear that Corin was neither aware of his extraordinary achievements in his ability to work, nor of his addiction to alcohol and how it affected him. That there is a 'flatness' in brain injury – a blankness – that makes drinking very comforting.

'What is the cause of my alcoholism?' Corin suddenly asked. Dr B said that would be difficult to answer and probably only he could, but again she reminded Corin of how he talked of growing up in an environment where drink was always on hand. In his words 'a reliable friend, in times of sadness or of happiness and success'. It was an unremarkable part of daily life – normal. Corin's resistance to acknowledging his problem with alcohol seems to come from his image of tramps covered in blankets, down by the Thames Embankment, drinking meths. Michael's drinking was glamorous to him. 'I remember my father taking me to this very smart wine shop in St James' Street. Berry Brothers...' and his face softened and brightened as he spoke about it. 'I'd like to go there again...'

Corin then remembered that we had both recently re-seen *Time Without Pity*, a film by Joseph Losey, made in protest against capital punishment. In the programme notes Losey had made some startling remarks about Michael Redgrave which has struck Corin greatly.

> It's unbelievably stupid that anybody, any society, could any longer believe that human beings have the right to take the lives of other human beings, under any circumstances. It's incomprehensible to me. I was making an English picture. It was very cheap, there was no question of the black list for the first time; it was the first picture on which I'd put my name in all that time. We were very limited on budget. But all those pictures: I was able to do them as well as I wanted, however well that was, and to have resources for them because in every case I could interest an actor who brought money and seriousness. In this case it was principally Redgrave and McKern. Redgrave is a great actor. He also did a wonderful job in *The Go-Between*. And I like him immensely, personally. And his gifts are more than acting: he's an intellectual, a poet, a literary man, an innovator in the theatre. But he's completely destroyed by alcohol. And even at that time there were one or two days when he was actually alcoholic. It was a big problem. But one of the remarkable things about him, and this is something every actor will understand and agree with, is that he never ever drank when he was playing a drunk.

At the end of the session we talked more about memory. Dr B asked Corin, 'Does it upset you not to have memories of your life together with Kika?' 'No, not really, it's strange…' She explained that he does *have* the memory but it can't always be accessed as the route to it, the cells which encode and retrieve memory, have been damaged. So the diary or notebook must be his prompt and that it can help him in just the same way as his glasses help him to see.

Later that night in bed, I remorselessly continue.

'…so I've got all the memories of us – and you have none. You don't know anything of me at all.'

'Oh yes I do…' He's getting sleepy.

'But I suppose I don't really know much about *you* now, you've come back so different… SO perhaps, perhaps… we have more in common than we thought. We've both got to begin learning about one another all over again. Do you think?' But he was asleep. Some things *don't* change.

CHAPTER TWENTY-FOUR

APRIL 2010
Goodbye

Corin's diary

To all in the world who listen and like to hear the truth
– even if it is uncomfortable and painful – I am Corin...
married to Kika... Redgrave. And that is my only claim to
happiness. My dear, good, absolutely beautiful wife. Without
her... I would have nothing. With her... I have... everything!!!

As time went on we grew bolder. We took more risks. Corin was
asked to perform *De Profundis* at the Irish Institute in Paris. I didn't
feel I was up to the challenge of accompanying Corin to Paris, given
the allure of the bars and restaurants, but didn't want to deny him
the chance of going – work meant so very much to him, especially
that work. And our friend Merlin Holland would be there. It was
wonderful, therefore, that Colin Chambers, who had worked with
Richard Nelson and Corin on the Wilde, offered to take Corin with
the help of our good friend Steve Tiller. Of course it was a risk. Corin
could have died at any time. Every time he took the tube alone it was
a risk. But they all came back in one piece and later, in an even more
daring venture, Steve took Corin to Finland to do a play reading of
Jim Allen's brilliant and controversial play *Perdition*. That, too, was
successfully managed by Steve.

For some time now Corin had grown much more independent,
and was having Alexander Technique lessons at the National with Sue

Laurie, travelling there and back by himself. He was seeing an analyst once a week in Chalk Farm, sometimes stopping before or after at The Enterprise, the big pub on the corner and often having lunch with Jemma, which he loved. He was also starting to see a counsellor in the alcoholic unit at Springfield and seemed to be getting better.

Corin's diary

January 2010

I have been making Arden worry about the amount I have been drinking. Last night I never got to Greg and Barbara's, as I had planned to do, to watch TV. I am determined to take charge of myself, with some real discipline, to stop this habit of drinking morning, noon and night.

I shall start today. I don't promise not to drink a single drop today. But both in the time (times) and especially in the amount I drink. I shall start today to be careful. To be normal. Not extravagant.

I promise myself and the family.

Jodie and Harvey's baby arrived on 10 January 2010; another January baby like Vanessa and Jemma. We were all perched around the high hospital bed. Jacquie, Tom, me, Corin, Arden, Jemma and Alfie, and took it in turns to hold little Edie, who put up with this effusion of love, pride and astonishment remarkably well.

Just before Easter we had a lovely visit at Chilham with Jacquie and Tom Reed and Harvey and Jodie. Corin was tired when we got home and went to bed early. I said good night to him and we said we loved each other, which we did nearly every night. An hour later I heard a strange noise and ran upstairs to find him trying to get round the bed and struggling to keep upright. I got him to the bed and could see him losing consciousness. I shouted to Arden, and he came at once and we tried to keep Corin awake while I called an ambulance. It could have happened any time and anywhere. I try to console myself with the miraculous fact that he was at home and that both Arden and I were with him, and he was never alone.

The paramedics were wonderful <u>again</u>, and we travelled to St George's behind the ambulance. From that moment on Corin never regained consciousness. He was in too fragile a state to have any tests or intervention, and by the time they had stabilised him it was too late to have made a significant operation: he had an aneurism that had bled into the brain. I could have insisted that they operated, but the doctors advised he would have had no quality of life whatsoever. I couldn't make that decision, so the family made it for me. He would be allowed to die naturally. That I had to give the 'yes' to no intervention still haunts and distresses me. Harvey and Arden tried to console me by assuring me Corin wouldn't have wanted to be helpless and might have preferred not to have been saved the first time around. But still... he had been getting so much better.

We kept a vigil for a week – me, Luke, Arden, Jemma, Tim, Alfie, Gabe, Jodie and Harvey – and many friends came, we played music and read to him. Harvey and I camped on the floor at night. Oliver, my nephew, was a great comfort. Harvey and I had gone home to get a shower and change of clothes when we had a call to say hurry back, but we got stuck in slow traffic. By the time we got there he had died without me. I understood. Sort of. He didn't feel free to go while I was there. He knew I couldn't bear to see him stop breathing. I saw it as a kindness to me. Corin looked like Thomas Chatterton, pale and beautiful – resting quietly. I asked to be alone with him and I told him how proud I was of him and how much I loved him, and would for the rest of my life. It was so comforting being with him I wanted to take him home. An hour later Lynn and Annabel arrived. Lynn in a wheelchair pushed by Malcolm. She was desperately ill with cancer herself, but flew over from New York to see him one last time. We left them together, she holding his hand and gazing at him with a sweet, calm forlornness. Lynn later wrote:

> Arrived at the hospital and there were Malcolm and Harvey and Jodie and little Edie. We headed on in and there he lay, looking absolutely beautiful. Noble, happy, free. I kissed him – he still had some warmth, although his nose was cold. My dearest brother.

> …Gone peacefully, Jemma said. So peacefully. Letting go with an easy breath. Gently – suddenly.

Sorrow and remorse. Can there be sorrow without remorse? Yes there can, but I didn't find that out till later. We live with the fear of death, we make films about it, we write about it, we are told until we're blue in the face and nearly dead ourselves that it is *a natural* part of life, but nothing prepares us. We are educated in all matters of sex, love, parenting, eating, but we are without strategies when it comes to the thing that haunts us. In the last century people died much younger and more frequently and were laid out in the parlour, and so people were more used to living with the reality of death. Now, with all our technology, we are estranged from it.

Anger is part of grief, certainly in my mind. Dead people do not come back. When, as happened to me, the truth finally dawns it is like being suddenly alone in a desert... a cold emptiness that stretches to the horizon with no future in sight. And no past either...

From *Dear Austen* by Nina Bawden.

I read these words over and over.

CHAPTER TWENTY-FIVE

MAY 2010
Highgate Cemetery

UK Parliament Early Day Motion 1237 06.04.2010

That this House expresses profound sadness at the death of Corin Redgrave – recalls his life as a brilliant actor, peace campaigner, supporter of the downtrodden and man of enormous principle and generous character, and offers its condolences to all his family and many friends at the loss of such a fine man.

Victor, the sexton, showed me how to hold the urn, with two hands, one holding the lip as it was heavy, and difficult to pour in a straight line so that the ashes would fall into the freshly dug hole below. My hands remembered pouring corn into the hens' trough at Lear Cottage, secretly watched by my mother from the bedroom window (checking on my accuracy), and my heart seemed to stop. I was pouring my husband into the ground. I kept some back though, and Victor gave me a little box so I could keep some at home.

It had been raining but now there was a large patch of blue sky and the sun shone on the bright green turf newly laid by Victor. We stood in a circle. Tom Reed read some Marcus Aurelius, Malcolm Tierney spoke about a memory of Corin that involved trying to find a person who looked like a penguin. Merlin Holland spoke directly to Corin about the gift that his grandfather Oscar Wilde had given him, and how that had led to Corin and Merlin becoming friends. I read out something Corin had written about his conversation with a taxi driver. Petra read her poem about him. I cried. Petra held my hand. Vanessa provided two bottles of champagne and some plastic cups, we emptied a third of one bottle into the grave and then toasted him with the rest.

We hadn't planned it like this. We had arranged that we were going to die together. Well, not quite. In the game we played we were nearly always on a cliff top. We were getting ready to jump off together (we would be in our nineties). But, just as I've jumped off, he gets distracted: 'Oh darling, I wasn't ready. You went so quickly. I wasn't looking... I'll follow you in a second. Just got to make a quick call... Lucille... is that you?' Or, he loses his footing and goes first: 'Oh, Corin! Oh, God, I'm so sorry, I'll be right behind you.' Then to myself: 'Oh, gosh, he's fallen an awfully long way down, I can't even see him. I'll go after lunch when I've said goodbye to Peter.'

But now here I was in Highgate Cemetery – he'd gone and left me on my own. He had disappeared. Gone up in smoke. I was alone. Without a plan.

Back at home, I was upstairs in the bedroom. Thanks to Jodie's thoughtfulness everything looked fresh and clean, without a trace of the traumatic struggle of the last weeks. I looked out of the window. It must have been spring. The tree in the street was late coming out. A crow was cawing from the roof of the flats opposite.

'There goes the Balham Crow,' Corin would say.

Four Years Later

Some months after Corin had come home I thought he had miraculously recovered. I was playing the piano and singing 'My Time of Day', his favourite song from *Guys and Dolls*, and why I chose the title of this book. He came and stood behind me and put his hand on my shoulder and with his other hand very gently touched my hair. I held my breath and went on playing but after a few seconds he moved away.

This memory is as vivid now as at was then. I can reach it when I need to.

I have lost my familiar point of reference and now must make my own. I must convince myself it is criminal to waste my life because C is not here to share it. This takes patience and practice.

Corin always sent me a postcard from wherever he was working. I kept them all. In our absences, we would cheer each other up by planning our next adventure. The oldest, and most battered card was sent from somewhere in America. It's the one I like best.

Air Mail

So perhaps th[...]
where we'll stay - somewhere
between Porter and
wolfjaws

with all my love
darling girl
Cxxx

Kika Markham
London
ENGLAND

Paul Matthews
Sun Breaking Through Between Porter and Wolfjaws
oil on linen, 30" x 40"

191

Acknowledgements

There are no maps or guidebooks that can tell you what to do or how to live after a loved one vanishes into the unknown. We experienced a rare kindness both from friends and family, and often from complete strangers where we lived in Balham. 'Thank you' doesn't go very far on the page, but I hope this book will go some way towards expressing my gratitude to everybody that helped us, whether medically, financially or baking a cake.

My profound thanks go to the people who provided outstanding care on the NHS: Dr Shai Betteridge, Professor Roger Kirby, Professor Mike Kopelman, Dr Paul Nicholas, the paramedics from Basildon and St George's Hospital, Ricky, the staff car park attendant at St Thomas' Hospital; and Adrian Stoddard.

Thank you to the Actors' Benevolent Fund and the Royal Theatrical Fund for their generosity and support.

To Vanessa, who initiated Corin's memorable work on *De Profundis* with Richard Nelson, and held my hand so often during the difficult times.

Thank you to Richard Nelson, Mark Rylance, David Thacker, Donald Sartaine, Justin Hardy, Steve Tiller, Lisa and Helen from Feast Management, Jimmy McGovern, John Dove and Nick Waring, for your care of Corin and your work with him, which restored an important part of his world.

Thank you to those of you that stayed with me on the journey after Corin's death and without whom this book could not have been written.

Eluned Hawkins and Fiona Shand, my invaluable unofficial editors. Delyth Jones, Caroline Duthy, Anita Boos, Bill

Bingham, Dr Jim McKeith, Tom O'Gorman, Bina and Sead Taslaman, Vivian Yates, Susan Lewis, Sally Simmons, Annie Castledine, Lydia Stryk, Nina Bawden, Miranda Lee White, Greg Lanning, Barbara Dinham, Michele Zackheim, and Martha Papadakis – thank you.

Thank you to James Hogan my publisher, and to Andrew Walby my inspiring editor, and the whole Oberon team for their creative support.

Thank you to my agent and friend Faith Evans for her guidance and persistence.

And lastly, my special thanks to my friend and mentor Francis Wyndham, who gave me the confidence to go on with my writing, and to my sisters and children for their unflagging support and love.

Sources

Bawden, Nina, *Dear Austen*. London: Little Brown, 2005

Callow, Simon, 'Corin Redgrave: Obituary'. London: 2010

Croall, Jonathan, *Don't You Know There's a War On? Voices from the Home Front*. Stroud: Sutton Publishing, 2005

Guthrie, Tyrone, 'Letter to the Ministry of Labour'. London: Old Vic/ Sadler's Wells, 14 May 1942

Hazzard, Shirley, *The Transit of Venus*. London: Penguin, 1980

Laing, R.D., *The Politics of Family and Other Essays*. New York, Pantheon Books, 1971

Lenin, Vladimir Il'ich, *Collected Works: Volume 38*. New York: Lawrence & Wishart, 1976

Mitchell, Alex, *Come the Revolution: A Memoir*. Kensington, N.S.W.: University of New South Wales Press, 2011

Piketty, Thomas, *Capital in the Twenty-First Century*. Harvard: Harvard University Press, 2014

Redgrave, Corin. *Michael Redgrave: My Father*. London: Richard Books, 1995

Thompson, David, 'Programme Notes to *Anne and Muriel*'. London: BFI Documentation Unit, 2011

Trotsky, Leon, *The Revolution Betrayed*. New York: Pioneer Publishers, 1945

List of Plates

Frontispiece
Portrait of Corin Redgrave. Watercolour by Kika Markham.
p.26
Photograph of David Markham: Ernest Rodker.
p.177
Handwritten note to Kika Markham by Corin Redgrave.
pp.190-191
Postcard (front and back): Corin Redgrave; Photograph: photographer unknown.

Plate Section I
p.1. Photograph: Stephen Harrison.
p.2. *Top:* Still from the film *The Stars Look Down; Bottom:* Photograph: photographer unknown.
p.3. Photograph: Stephen Harrison.
p.4. *Top:* Photograph: Stephen Harrison; *Bottom:* Photograph: Kika Markham.
p.5. Photograph: Morris Newcombe/ArenaPAL.
p.6. *Top:* Photograph: Lord Snowdon; *Bottom:* Photograph: David Edwards. Copyright © BBC.
p. 7. Photographs: Pierre Zucca.
p.8. *Top:* Photograph: Pierre Zucca; *Bottom:* Photograph: Ernest Rodker

Plate Section II
p.1. *Top left:* Photograph: Corin Redgrave; *Top right:* Photograph: photographer unknown; *Bottom:* Photograph: Sean Hudson.
p.2. *Top left and inset:* Photographs: Fi Green; *Bottom:* Photograph: Kika Markham.
p.3. *Top and bottom:* Photographs: Kika Markham.
p.4. *Top:* Photograph copyright © Ivan Kyncl; *Bottom:* Photograph: taken by passer-by.
p.5. Photographer unknown.
pp.6, 7 & 8. Photographs: Kika Markham and family.

Index

Aamer, Shaker 170
Ahmad, Babar 76, 105
Allen, Jim 16, 182
Amoroso, Dr Peter 83-84, 89, 126
Armstrong-Jones, Antony, 1st Earl of
    Snowdon 28
Ashcroft, Peggy 9
Atkins, Eileen 115

B, Doctor 1, 3, 112, 132, 164, 176,
    178-180
Barnes, Clive 60
Barton, John 118
Battersby, Roy 30
Bawden, Nina 77, 186
Begg, Azmat 155
Bellow, Greg 13
Bellow, Saul 13
Bevan, Daisy 151
Bingham, Bill 80-81, 166
Blizzard, John 155
Blizzard, Vivian 155, 156
Bose, Mathew 61
Bostridge, Ian 156
Boyle, Danny 30
Brind, Tom 114, 151
Bukovsky, Vladimir 9
Burstein, Keith 169

Callow, Simon 28
Caron, Leslie 26
Castledine, Annie 58-59, 61, 99
Chalfant, Henry 65
Chalfant, Kathy 65
Chambers, Colin 182
Chaplin, Geraldine 27
Christian, Louise 77
Clark, Annabel 185
Clark, Kelly (Pema) 93, 100
Cookson, Cherry 97-98
Croall, Jonathan 8
Cronin, A.J. 6

de Menezes, Jean Charles 170
Dehn, Olive 36
Dehn, Paul 14, 93
Dinham, Barbara 82
Dove, John 172

Edmonds, Joe 114
Edwards, Percy 14
Ekbal, Doctor 83
el Khali, Zina 171
Evans, Harold 32
Fyles, Roz 70
Eyre, Peter 156

Feest, Alec 175
Ferguson, Alex 58
Fisk, Robert 171
Frears, Stephen 61

Garnett, Tony 14
Gentle, Rose 80
Goring, Marius 28
Guthrie, Tyrone 7-8

Hall, Peter 9
Hall Clark, Steve 30
Hamilton-Hill, Deirdre 19-20, 36, 41,
    115-116
Hardy, Justin 134-135
Hare, David 76-77
Harrison, Howard 9
Hawkins, Eluned 44
Healy, Gerry 19, 43
Herman, Victor 187
Hickman, Doctor 101, 103
Hofmeyr, Retha 120
Holland, Merlin 182, 187
Hollinghurst, Alan 136
Hughes, Doctor 123
Hughes, Simon 172
Hunter, Kathryn 82

Jellicoe, Ann 21
Johnson, Dilys 15
Johnstone, Keith 17
Jong, Hyu 153

Kavanaugh, Rachel 141
Kempinski, Tom 43
Kempson, Rachel 6
Kempson, Robin 120
Kenwright, Bill 61
Kirby, Professor Roger 67-70, 83, 87, 123, 178
Kopelman, Professor Michael 138-139, 175
Kossoko, Aicha 123
Kushner, Tony 59, 65, 175

Lafont, Bernadette 27
Lanning, Greg 183
Laurie, Sue 183
Lavery, Bryony 104, 166
Lawrence, Maureen 58
Léaud, Jean-Pierre 21
Leicester, Margot 39, 101
Lewenstein, Oscar 16, 21
Lloyd-Pack, Roger 123, 170
Loach, Ken 14
Losey, Joseph 180
Lowe, Doctor 82

McEwan, Doctor 90
MacKeith, Dr Jim 133
MacKeith, Gwen 139
MacKeith, Jim 70, 101
MacKeith, Jo (Frances) 11, 128
MacKeith, Keesje 139
Maggie, neighbour 82
Magni, Marcello 82
Mario, Doctor 75
Markham, David 6-9 36
Markham, Jehane 10, 18, 21, 41, 44, 50, 95, 119, 123, 135- 136, 148, 150
Markham, Petra 10, 17, 91, 95, 100
Markham, Sonia (Sonie) 10-11, 87, 95, 127, 149, 164
Marsden, Peter 158
Mercer, David 14, 17, 26
Merrison, Clive 27, 31, 42
Milne, A.A 9
Morley, Sheridan 61
Morris, Peter 137
Mullin, Chris 16-17
Murdoch, Iris 9

Naiambana, Patrice 82
Neeson, Liam 62
Neill, A.S. 11
Nelson, Richard 13, 76, 155-156, 182
Nero, Carlo 168
Nero, Franco 172-174
Nero, Jenny 168
Nero, Lily 168
Nunn, Sylvia 67, 69, 115
Nunn, Trevor 65, 156

O'Gorman, Tom 93, 120, 127, 142
O'Rourke, Josie 167
Ogier, Bulle 26
Osborne, John 21
Owen, Alfie 138, 165, 183-184
Owen, Gabe 138, 165, 184
Owen, Tim (son-in-law) 138, 184

Papini, Cristina 147
Pinter, Harold 9, 21, 70
Potter, Dennis 27
Puxon, Grattan 80

Quast, Phil 99

Ramsburg, Charlie 65, 75
Redgrave, Arden 41-42. 45, 47-49, 58
Redgrave, Edie 183, 185
Redgrave, Harvey 40, 44, 47- 49, 64, 81, 87, 95, 109-110, 117, 124, 151, 171, 183-185
Redgrave, Jemma 19, 36, 41, 81, 84, 90, 95-96, 109, 127, 134-135, 138, 140, 154, 162-165, 169, 183-185
Redgrave, Jodie 87, 109-110, 124, 151, 171, 183-184
Redgrave, Luke 6, 19, 36, 41, 81, 95, 102, 142-143, 184
Redgrave, Lynn 67, 90, 129
Redgrave, Michael 6-7, 12, 42, 61, 149, 172, 180
Redgrave, Vanessa 16, 58, 61-62, 65, 67, 91, 101-102, 107-108, 114-115, 118, 120-122, 126, 129, 155, 172- 174, 176, 183, 187
Reed, Jacquie 151, 183
Reed, Tom 151, 183, 187
Reich, Wilhelm 13, 42

Reisz, Betsy 18
Reisz, Karel 18
Richardson, Joely 151
Richardson, Natasha 16, 91, 172
Richardson, Tony 16
Rivette, Jacques 27
Robbins, Professor Ian 122
Roché, Henri-Pierre 32
Rodker, Ernest 164
Rodker, Oliver 184
Rubens, Bernice 15
Russell, Bertrand 13
Russell, Shirley 44
Rylance, Mark 94-95, 105, 107, 134

Sartain, Donald 58
Schiffman, Suzanne 21-23, 25, 49, 72
Scott, Liz 175
Serbedzija, Rade 58
Simmonds, Sally 49, 59, 82, 93, 130
Smith, Roger 14, 30, 43
Soames, Robin, 137
Soans, Robin, 154
Stack, Suzannah 151
Stafford-Clark, Max 76-77
Steiner, George 9
Stokes, Kate 64

Taslaman, Bina 81, 127
Taslaman, Sead 81, 127
Taslaman, Vedran 119
Tendeter, Stacey 21
Thacker, David 58
Thatcher, Margaret 29, 33, 136
Thomas, Polly 137
Tierney, Andrea 104
Tierney, Malcolm 18, 26, 58, 155, 185,
    187
Tiller, Steve 182
Trodd, Ken 27
Truffaut, François 9, 21,
Tynan, Ken 13

van den Broek, Dr Martin 117
Voikhanskaya, Marina 100, 138

Waite, Terry 100
Waring, Nick 172
Warner, David 17
West, Jehane 18
Wilson, Barbara 103
Wilson, Sue 141
Winterbottom, Michael 14
Wyndham, Francis 28, 156, 193

Zackheim, Michele 65, 75

www.oberonbooks.com

Follow us on www.twitter.com/@oberonbooks
& www.facebook.com/oberonbook